In Action with Destroyers
1939–1945

Dedicated to Johnny Lee-Barber
Captain and friend who saved the lives of so many of us

In Action with Destroyers 1939–1945

The Wartime Memoirs of Commander J A J Dennis DSC RN

Anthony Cumming

Pen & Sword
MARITIME

First published in Great Britain in 2017 by
PEN & SWORD MARITIME
an imprint of
Pen & Sword Books Ltd
47 Church Street
Barnsley
South Yorkshire
S70 2AS

ISBN 978 1 52671 849 5

A CIP catalogue record for this book is
available from the British Library.

Printed and bound in England by TJ International Ltd, Padstow, PL28 8RW.

Pen & Sword Books Ltd incorporates the Imprints of Pen & Sword
Archaeology, Atlas, Aviation, Battleground, Discovery, Family History,
History, Maritime, Military, Naval, Politics, Railways, Select, Transport,
True Crime, Fiction, Frontline Books, Leo Cooper, Praetorian Press,
Seaforth Publishing, Wharncliffe and White Owl.

For a complete list of Pen & Sword titles please contact
PEN & SWORD BOOKS LIMITED
47 Church Street, Barnsley, South Yorkshire, S70 2AS, England
E-mail: enquiries@pen-and-sword.co.uk
Website: www.pen-and-sword.co.uk

Contents

Acknowledgements

Bringing Alec's memoirs to a wider readership has involved the cooperation and willing assistance of a great many individuals. I would like to thank the staff of the Imperial War Museum, London, where I discovered his memoir in 2006. In particular I must thank Mr Roderick Suddaby, Keeper of the Department of Documents and, more recently, Maria Payne for contacting Alec's children, Charity Reddington and Alan Dennis, of British Columbia, Canada. This allowed me to confirm their copyright status as proprietors of their father's papers after his death in 2008. My relationship with Charity and Alan has been very rewarding and I consider myself extremely fortunate to have gained their trust and friendship. Many of the photographs have come from their family album and the ultimate success of this project will be the result of their commitment and respect for their father's memory. Sadly, Charity's husband Graham died during the production of this book and we owe him a tremendous debt of gratitude for all the support he gave us. Alan has made it clear throughout that they have always kept in mind what their father would have wanted and both have generously agreed that after expenses have been paid, royalties from the book should go to the charity Help for Heroes. This organisation was founded to help provide better facilities for British service men and women wounded or injured in the line of duty. We all owe them an enormous debt of gratitude that we can never adequately repay.

Grateful thanks go to Nick Knollys and Willow Ellis for their kind permission to use their father's superb warship paintings, especially of *Griffin* for the dust jacket. As this image shows, Alec's former Dartmouth classmate, the late

Lieutenant Commander Hugh Knollys DSC, was not just a brave and successful naval officer but also a talented artist.

Others have also played crucial roles, including Canadian war veteran and Alec's great friend, the late Frank Wade, who first encouraged him to write the memoir. Furthermore, without John Somerville's suggestion that the papers be placed within the Imperial War Museum's archive, I would probably never have known of them.

I am also obliged to Professor G.H. (Harry) Bennett and Commander David Hobbs RN who took time to look at the manuscript and make constructive suggestions for my editorial contribution. We are also indebted to Christopher Somerville for his kind words supporting Alec's work. Grateful thanks also go to James W. Smith, PhD candidate, Kings College, London, and old friends Mark Vidler and history teacher Graham Ward for their continuing encouragement. I am also indebted to everyone at Pen & Sword for their patience, help, and guidance, especially for Editor Henry Wilson's firm hand on the tiller, but also to Matt Jones for technical assistance with the maps and images and Barnaby Blacker, who copy-edited everything with skill and sensitivity.

Last, but not least, thanks go to my wife Sarah for her patience and encouragement over the past year. Any mistakes that remain in transposing Alec's text or in my own contributions are entirely my own responsibility.

Anthony J. Cumming,
Paignton.

Foreword

Naval historians have a number of ways in which they may gain insight into their subject. Although war diaries and ships' logs provide hard evidence of the operations ships were involved in, they shed too little light on why individuals acted as they did under the strain of prolonged periods at sea in action. An autobiographical story written with clarity by someone who took part in some of the most significant actions can take the reader into some of the most important and challenging naval operations of World War II and build up an awareness of how those taking part felt. *In Action with Destroyers* by Commander Alec Dennis, edited by Anthony J Cumming, is just such a book. The author served in the destroyers GRIFFIN and SAVAGE and saw action off Norway, Crete, Madagascar and in several of the Arctic Convoys. It is written in a candid style that makes the reader aware of how relentless attack from aircraft and U-boats could have an impact on morale but how the training and discipline of a ship's company could shine through and allow them to take on almost anything, even against enormous odds, with cheerfulness and courage. This book adds a human dimension to the many published histories of the war at sea and is strongly recommended as an important addition to the bibliography of the war at sea.

Commander David Hobbs RN
7 April 2017

Maps

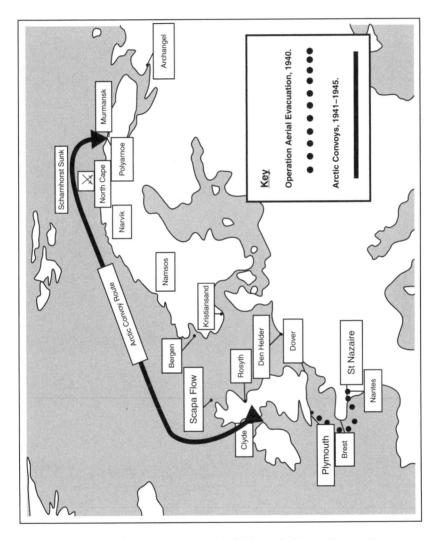

Map 1 – Map of Operation Aerial, 1940, and the main arctic convoy route, 1941–45.

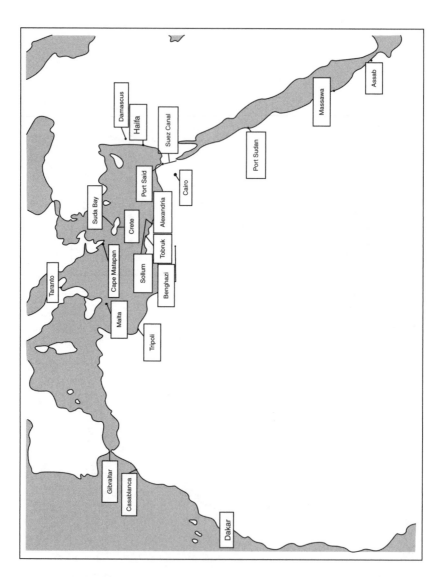

Map 2 – The Mediterranean and Red Sea.

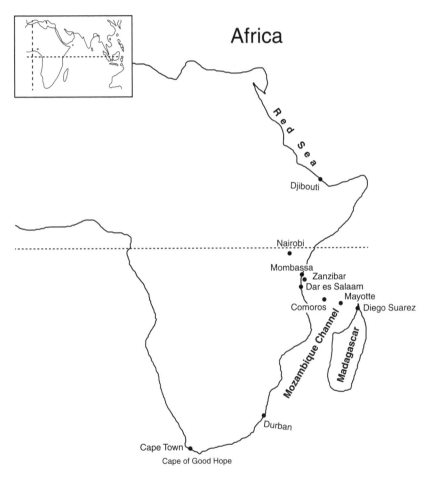

Map 3 – The Madagascar Operation, 1942.

Editor's Introduction

'If the Dons sight Devon, I'll quit the port o' Heaven,
An' drum them up the Channel as we drumm'd them
long ago.'

Sir Henry Newbolt[1]

To my great regret, I never met Alec Dennis face to face
though I had read his war memoirs in the reading room of the
Imperial War Museum, London. Sadly, Alec is no longer with
us and though he never wrote his experiences for commercial
gain, they are a fascinating eyewitness account from one of
the most heavily dive-bombed naval officers fighting many
crucial naval battles of the Second World War. At least I
managed to strike up an e-mail relationship with him, the
memories of which remain with me to the present day. Over
the course of a year, we had many stimulating discussions
ranging from the ability of warships to withstand air attack
to his pre-war experience as a naval cadet at Britannia Royal
Naval College, Dartmouth in Devon, an establishment close
to where I live and with which I retain some connections.

These conversations originated from my request to the
Imperial War Museum for clearance to quote some of Alec's
anecdotes for my first book. I then received his amusing
letter:

'You certainly have my permission to quote
anything from that memo except for some rather
unsubstantiated criticisms of my elders and betters
and the couple of times I had a bit too much to drink.'

Until then I had not even considered the possibility of Alec
still living so was thrilled to discover he was alive and well,
age 88, residing in Vancouver, Canada, and happy to discuss
his wartime experiences via e-mail. Later, he posted me a
bound volume of these papers, a generous act that has driven
me to present his work to a wider audience. His memoirs
cover a brief but idyllic period of travel and recreation in
the Far East during 1938, through to some of the fiercest
campaigns of the Second World War around the world. For
Alec, the European campaign ended with the surrender of
the German forces at Kristiansand, Norway. His friend, John
Somerville (son of the famous admiral), later encouraged
him to lodge the original memoir with the Imperial War
Museum for the benefit of future scholars. About three years
later, Alec had fifty copies bound and printed for the benefit
of family, friends, and people with naval backgrounds
and it was only then that his family was able to gain some
understanding of his wartime service. Like many of his
generation, Alec found it difficult to speak to family about
wartime experiences and it was probably easier to commit
traumatic memories to paper than talk in detail about them.
I felt immensely honoured to receive one of the last few
remaining copies.

Alec's wartime career was in destroyers – small, nimble
and fast in comparison with the Royal Navy's capital ships
but cramped and uncomfortable with a bridge open to the
elements. As Rear Admiral D. Arnold-Forster wrote, 'It
is in the small craft ... that the spirit of adventure thrives
best, for small ships penetrate where big ships cannot. And
in the destroyer service especially there is an element of
daring and glamour that appeals to those with strong sea
instincts.'[2] Sadly, there were rarely enough of these warships
to go around in the Second World War. This was particularly
true in the period before destroyers became available from
the United States in 1941 when 'every destroyer was worth
her weight in gold'.[3] The destroyer's role was to attack, yet
in the Second World War, they also defended other ships

from many forms of enemy attack. Indeed, providing one was available, no larger warship ever put to sea without a destroyer acting as a chaperon.[4]

Readers should take into account that Alec wrote his memoirs when attitudes to people from developing countries were different and he used terms that writers would avoid today. The wisdom of novelist L.P. Hartley holds that 'The past is a foreign country; they do things differently there.' As his daughter later confirmed, 'Dad had a wicked sense of humour' and this shines through in his writing. He admitted, 'It is being written without much revision, directly from memory, assisted by some scraps of paper, navigator's notebooks and appointment calendars, which have survived many moves.' Indeed, it seems that post-war writers, in particular Winston Churchill's multi-volume *The Second World War* and official historian Captain Stephen Roskill's *The War at Sea*, have influenced the text to some extent. At the same time, Alec has also assisted contemporary and well-known authors such as Simon Sebag-Montefiore and Ronald Spector.[5] In spite of the obvious limitations of such a personal record, this book allows a wider audience to appreciate this wartime sailor's vivid and personal experiences in the broader context of the war at sea.

At times, one can almost hear the scream of the bombs; feel the leap of the deck as they explode nearby and experience his gut-tearing tension as the ship moves through minefields and U-boat-infested waters. In such circumstances, high-spirited young men need outlets to dissipate the strain that accumulates when forced to endure extreme situations and readers can expect many amusing anecdotes and colourful episodes during off-duty moments. There are also numerous human insights into the personalities of those caught up in these momentous events. As such, his narrative is one that will appeal more to the educated general reader than an academic professor, but the serious student of military history will find his words fascinating.

Part I

The End of Peace and the Phoney war

Prewar

I have never had the urge to keep a diary but we were obliged by their Lordships of the Admiralty to keep a journal during our time as midshipmen. My journal ceases abruptly on the day on which it was to be assessed as part of our examination in seamanship for sub-lieutenant. After finishing these examinations onboard HMS *Adventure*, Hugh Knollys, Hugh Wilson, and I left HMS *Suffolk* and had ten days to spare in Hong Kong before boarding the Blue Funnel liner *Hector* for the passage back to England. We would normally have been accommodated in the naval base HMS *Tamar* since the *Suffolk* was to go North; but fortunately a chance remark at a party resulted in a handsome offer from the District Officer of the Northern Territories to make use of his house at Taipo while he was away. This turned out to be a wholly delightful experience. The house was on a small peninsula not far from the Chinese border. A boat, a car, and a staff of attentive domestics were on hand. On rising in the morning, showers were ready running at the right temperature, toothpaste ready spread on the brush and clothes laid out on the bed before dressing for breakfast and a carefree day. After this last taste of the old regime in the Far East, we three embarked in the *Hector* on March 9 for the six-week passage home.

This was a most agreeable time. *Hector* was a cargo liner carrying about 150 passengers. Each port on the long Imperial route produced its own brand of people. At Hong Kong, we already had businessmen and their ladies returning from

Japan and Shanghai, together with a handful of Service people like ourselves – commanders and the like, and one brigadier who spent much of the voyage half-naked in the sun, doing embroidery under the watchful eye of his wife. Presumably, she wouldn't let him loose among the several young wives who were taking a break from the Orient, leaving their husbands behind.

At Singapore, the first port of call, I decided to leave the ship and travel by train to Penang where I hoped to meet her again. Although the Navy allows one to see much of the world, one seldom gets a chance to travel inland, and I wanted to see more of Malaya. It was just as well because it turned out to be a last glimpse of that part of the Empire before the coming catastrophe – which, I may say, we fully expected, having seen the mood of the Japanese and our own pathetic weakness in that part of the world. I had a look at the naval base, which had just been declared open. A fine base – but no fleet, and therefore untenable. The train took me to Kuala Lumpur, where I spent a couple of days and took a car trip through Klang to Port Swettenham. This, naturally, cost more than I expected and I began to run short of money, resorting to a staple diet of bananas and coconut. The latter sticks to my throat to this day. However, I survived and arrived at last at the rail terminus opposite Penang. Arose at dawn to cross in a ferry on a wonderful pearl-grey tropical morning – warm and flat calm. Spent a day in Penang looking at temples and swimming; then saw *Hector* arrive and joined her again before she sailed.

Then to Colombo (where *Hector* was sunk by Nagumo's carriers almost exactly four years later). A new crop of passengers – tea planters this time; a slightly less rowdy lot than the rubber planters from Singapore. At each port, time for a 'run ashore' and a swim but not much more. Thence back along the 'all red' route – Aden, Suez, Port Said, Malta, Gibraltar – with a skip up to Marseilles to allow the eager ones to get home a few days earlier by train, and others to avoid the Bay of Biscay. In the event, the passage from

Gibraltar was rather rough. I felt queasy as usual (I never really got over seasickness) and, not being liable to keep a watch, tried a fair amount of brandy and soda which didn't help at all. At last arrived at Tilbury – a dreary mud flat up the Thames. But it was home and good to be back. I had started reading *Gone with the Wind* as we left Hong Kong and arrived at Tilbury at the beginning of the last chapter. To this day, I have never finished it.

1938

After suitable leave at home I started the usual sub-lieutenant's courses at Portsmouth: gunnery, torpedo, signals, navigation and (an innovation) a 'war course', which I greatly enjoyed as it had to do with strategy and staff work rather than the technicalities of the other courses. A memory, which remains, is that of an address by the formidable Admiral of the Fleet, the Earl of Cork and Orrery (for short – Ginger Boyle) who held forth about the Offensive Spirit in war. Only two years later, as shall be seen, we came across him at sea in Norway, his offensive spirit thoroughly frustrated by muddle and bad direction from above. A story I always liked concerning him had it that his successor, Admiral Sir Roger Backhouse, under whose earnest rule I had served as a midshipman, was attending ceremonial Sunday Divisions in his flagship when a seagull chose to drop its mess on the deck just in front of him. A gnarled commissioned gunner was heard to say: 'That would never have happened in Lord Cork's time.'

Having the right type of brain for these courses, I didn't have to exert myself unduly to achieve six 'firsts', and was able to have the usual fun available to impecunious sub-lieutenants, including a used Wolseley Hornet motor-car, which my father said, quite rightly, I would never be able to afford to run. However, it did me quite well until a collision obliged me to leave it (pending enough income to repair it) in a corner of HM Dockyard where it was ultimately destroyed by the German Air Force, along with the summons (arising out of the collision), which went up in flames in the Portsmouth Guildhall.

To our disappointment, the traditional civilizing course at the Royal Naval College, Greenwich, had to be dropped because of the obvious approach of war and the need to get us to sea again as soon as possible. This was sad because apart from the non-naval content of the courses – history, languages, and so forth – Greenwich was so handy to London that one could go to parties there and still be back in time for one's duties in the morning. However, we managed pretty well at Portsmouth.

It wasn't long before the imminence of war made itself felt directly. In September 1938 arose the Munich crisis. Whatever the rest of the country felt, most of us were ready and willing to fight right then. And into our classrooms came some rather dramatic developments. From time to time, an officer would appear, call for one of us by name, and hand him his appointment. So we were scattered to various ports and harbours in Britain – and, indeed, further afield. One fortunate group joined the liner *Aquitania* and went out to Egypt where they were to man certain barges in the Suez Canal. However, the crisis was over by the time they got there, and all they had to worry about was their bar bill.

In a pedestrian version of the Duchess of Richmond's ball, I was tapped on the shoulder and told to report to Devonport Dockyard as sub-lieutenant of HMS *Sturdy*, a small destroyer built in the First World War. She was lying in the bottom of a dry dock being pulled out of reserve as fast as possible. Her Captain was already there, a delightful Lieutenant Commander called Ben Barker, a well-known destroyer character. (In May 1997 Ben's son Captain Nick Barker died. At the time of the Falklands crisis in 1982, he was Captain of HMS *Endurance* in Antarctica. *Sturdy* herself was wrecked in a storm on the West Coast of Scotland in 30 October, 1940).

Ben Barker later perished most gallantly in the *Ardent* while trying to defend the *Glorious* against the *Scharnhorst* and *Gneisenau*. Why he didn't get the Victoria Cross I do not know except there were hardly any survivors on our side and they were in prisoner of war camps, so no reports were received until after the war.

In the *Sturdy* we were fairly busy, but a great deal of gin was drunk, particularly as Ben had found some stockbrokers who had been recalled from civilian life, most of them having been 'axed' in the 1920s by the infamous Mr. Geddes. They were, one and all, happy to be back with duty-free gin and no careers to worry about. Among other useful accomplishments, I was taught how to chew broken glass. However, we had no sooner got the ship seaworthy than the crisis was over – or rather postponed in an inglorious way. I was in two minds: partly disappointed, but also somewhat relieved because the *Sturdy* was a horribly uncomfortable little bucket with no modern equipment and we could hardly have been employed on other than secondary duties. I am sure I should have been deadly seasick much of the time.

One of the appurtenances of my cabin was a tin bath, which hung on three hooks suspended from the deckhead. The bath was wider than the hatch down to the cabin flat, so the ship had been built around it.

So then, we all went back to our studies again, to be faced almost at once with an examination in Signals. But a sympathetic Chief Yeoman gave us all the questions beforehand so that everyone got over 90 per cent, a suspicious circumstance, which caused the authorities to have us repeat the test under more stringent scrutiny. Our curtailed courses came to an end before Christmas and after a short spell of leave I embarked at Southampton in the *Nevasa*, an ex-P&O ship in which my parents had once travelled to India. She was now a troopship and not very comfortable. But the passage was short and by the end of January 1939, I disembarked in Malta to join the destroyer *Griffin*, First Destroyer Flotilla; she was an immense improvement on the *Sturdy* and a really going concern. I was to stay in her nearly four years.

Griffin

She was lying in Sliema Creek, the destroyer harbour and home for four destroyer flotillas totalling some thirty-five boats, all modern and in very good shape except for one glaring defect, which would cause much grief later: most of them were all virtually defenceless against determined air attack. However, at this time they looked splendid, clean, smart, and efficient. I was introduced to Lieutenant Commander Johnny Lee-Barber, the captain, who lent me some civilian clothes to go ashore in, until my baggage arrived. We had the inevitable gin, and I felt closely appraised. Soon I met the rest of the wardroom – only six officers in those days, including the captain. Tony Juniper was the first lieutenant: dark, saturnine, efficient, and charming though rather nervous in manner; wife French and delightful. The No. 2, Kenneth Letts, was a 'rocky turnover'; that is, an ex-reserve officer from the Merchant Service who had turned over to the Royal Navy fairly recently due to the great expansion which was just starting. I thought him a little 'rough' (we were very snobbish, I suppose) but nice enough and a competent navigator.

The 'Chief' (engineer officer) was a most smooth character, Robin Rampling, whom I never got to know very well as he went sick not long after the start of the war and was relieved by Jack Fenn-Clark. Lastly, and far from least, was the gunner (T), Florrie Foord, one of the most wonderful men that the Navy could produce. I am eternally grateful to him for holding my hand in the days when I was wet behind the ears. My predecessor, Peter Black, had a pronounced stammer in times of stress and I wondered how he managed as officer of the watch at high speed. But he seems to have overcome his difficulty and the only thing that bothered him about the turnover was whether his farewell party went well. It did. A good proportion of the flotilla wardrooms attended, including George Creasy, our admirable captain (D).

The following day was my first as Officer of the Day; inevitable because 18 February 1939 was Carnival Day in Malta and I was of course junior boy. Unfortunately it was also my 21st birthday, so I had to comfort myself with a bottle of champagne (*Griffin* had recently visited Marseille) and some Beethoven on the excellent radiogram presented to the wardroom by the ship's builders. Later that evening I was half-asleep in one of the armchairs awaiting the return of the captain, as one could not turn in until he had been met. At last the quartermaster clattered down the ladder and reported:

'Captain returning on board, sir.'

I went up on deck to see nothing but a dghaisa (a small gondola-type boat common in Malta), empty but for the dghaisaman.

'I don't see the captain anywhere, quartermaster.'

'He was there, sir.'

A moment later, Johnny appeared swimming strongly towards the ladder. I suppose he had fallen backwards out of the dghaisa when the boatman gave a last heave of his oars. Quite unruffled, JLB came up the ladder in wet mess undress.

'Evening, sub.'

He disappeared into the wardroom bathroom for a hot bath. He was still there in the morning.

I found myself to be the correspondence officer, sharing a hot little office next to the engine room with Able Seaman Sprague, the office writer, a big typewriter, a safe and a lot of files. Sprague had huge hands and punished the typewriter with great gusto so that the full stop went right through six copies as a hole in the paper. As Their Lordships had arranged courses on every subject except correspondence, I found myself somewhat at sea. Johnny treated correspondence with apparent disdain, but had an eye like a hawk for what mattered so that one had to be careful before getting him to sign anything. One also had responsibility for the confidential books and documents, the loss of one page of any of which could result in a board of enquiry. On one occasion, I left the keys in the safe when summoned in a hurry for some such emergency as a senior officer passing by in a boat, to be presented with them by Sprague with a completely deadpan expression. I was also Torpedo Control Officer and kept one watch in three at sea with Letts and Florrie Foord, Tony Juniper taking a standing morning watch as was customary for first lieutenants.

In less than a week, the fleet left Malta for the spring combined manoeuvres with the Home Fleet. These took place annually from Gibraltar and represented a busy and exciting time both professionally with demanding exercises and socially with the rather alcoholic get-togethers with one's opposite numbers in the Home Fleet. There were exercises all the way to Gib. To begin with, I was only an understudy on watch as I had yet to earn a watchkeeping certificate. This award was at the discretion of the captain who had to judge nicely how safe you were on your own without interfering unless you were positively dangerous. Perfect station keeping was demanded in any formation. As we were the junior ship, we were last in line of nine, so sometimes a sort of concertina effect made life rather difficult. You could be sure that the captain would arrive on the bridge just as you were either miles behind or far too close to your next ahead, and either going like hell to catch up or virtually stopped and still gaining on her. It turned out that in wartime one was not often at sea in line ahead; but it was a good test of nerve and judgement, especially at high speed at night.

We spent a couple of weeks in March in and out of Gibraltar. The fleet exercises were planned in great – perhaps too great – detail and called for many reports and post-mortems. I had some difficulty getting Johnny to sign any of the papers as he was always either on the bridge, ashore, busy, turned in or entertaining. I felt like the anxious secretary of some eastern potentate. However, what had to be done got done, and at sea I began to realise that we were in the hands of a master of the craft. We didn't spend much time in harbour, but one day I was bidden to the 'Mount', the residence of the Rear

Admiral, Gibraltar, who at the time was Ned Evans, brother of my aunt Marjorie Strange. I found myself talking to a greying, short man dressed in a rather scruffy suit, looking a bit like a dockyard man. In a rather condescending way, I asked him what he did. It turned out that he was Ralph Kerr, Captain (D), Second Destroyer Flotilla, one of our rivals. At least I learned a bit from that 'sermon on the mount'. He was later killed as captain of the *Hood* in her last fight with the *Bismarck*. Ned Evans, too, was killed in an aircraft flying from Canada to England during the war.

After those exercises, we returned to Malta, continuing to exercise for the duration of the trip and as well most days once we arrived there. It was clear that war was only a matter of time so we shipped warheads on our torpedoes and primed depth charges and shells. One night we were out as a flotilla doing a mock torpedo attack at high speed. This was a most thrilling business; all ships darkened, the ship ahead just visible by her dark shape and a little blue light over her white wake. We were in quarterline at thirty knots in close order – a cable and a half apart – when a dim light flashed ordering a course change to starboard. Unfortunately, one ship (*Glowworm*, I think) turned the wrong way. There was a noise like a hundred car crashes and showers of sparks as she scraped down the side of the next ship, narrowly missing her torpedo warheads, which were trained on the beam. I heard Johnny say, 'Lord, what a crumbles,' as we turned clear to see what help was needed. Luckily no one was hurt, though both ships had to be docked for repairs.

There was a Board of 'Iniquity' but the Admiral quite firmly took a 'no omelettes' attitude, and that was that. We all felt better for the decision. We had not been long in Malta before the next drama. It was Sunday, 7 April 1939. Being dogsbody, I had the duty of marching the Roman Catholic church party to mass ashore. I had a pleasant wait in a café until they came out again, and then marched them back to find a scene of great activity. Awnings were being furled, cables unshackled from buoys, boilers lit up and boats everywhere. The signal said, 'Raise steam for full speed. Prepare for sea. Report when ready to proceed.' Mussolini had invaded Albania. Johnny L-B and the captain of the *Zulu* were ashore on Manoel lsland mating their bull-terriers – Johnny's 'Jamie', pure white, with *Zulu*'s 'Daisy', a brindle bitch. There was an agonizing delay as they were *in flagrante delicto* and it took a while to part them until the coxswain of the boat got a bucket of water and saved the situation.

So off to Alexandria we went. I found it a fascinating place. The approach from the sea is difficult, the shore-line flat and of a uniform ochre colour with few distinguishing marks. Sometimes in hazy weather you could locate the city in a general way from the smell – a mixture of raw sewage and tannery effluent. The harbour entrance is by way of a narrow channel called the Great Pass, marked at the seaward end by 'Drunken Beacon'. This pass made the harbour rather vulnerable to mining or blocking and became the object of much attention in the next few months. Once inside, the harbour is quite spacious.

The destroyers berthed inside an ancient breakwater at the inner end of which was Tas el Tin lighthouse and one of King Farouk's palaces. A little to the east lay the remains of the ancient Pharos, giving an overwhelming feeling of the past. One went ashore by felucca if the ship's boat was not available, then walked through a poor and sordid area before one came to the civilized part of the city. This was very civilized and, given enough money, one need want for nothing. Even on a sub-lieutenant's pay, I did pretty well as we were honorary members of the Union Club and the Sporting Club, with recreation of all kinds from horseracing to squash. In addition, I found that the uncle of one of my cousins, a retired British Admiral, was now Director of Ports and Lights for Egypt. He looked well in a tarbush and owned a dahabiya near Ras el Tin from which one could swim and climb back on board among the iced drinks, Sudanese servants and expatriate English girls. I don't suppose anyone ever took a coliform count of the harbour water, but in spite of all the drains of the Middle East I only got a bad ear and the usual gippy tummy which affects all new arrivals.

In fact, we worked pretty hard and spent a lot of time at sea doing exercises of every kind. In between there were regular patrols up and down and outside the Great Pass, particularly when Italian merchant ships were using it. I don't think we would have been caught in a 'Pearl Harbor' because we were always conscious that there might be a surprise attack. At that time the Italians, though undoubtedly hostile, were something of an unknown quantity. Although they hadn't much of a fighting record, their larger ships and aircraft were much more modern than ours. And our anti-aircraft capability was pathetic. When we had the occasional shoot at a radio-controlled 'Queen Bee' aircraft, the target used to fly straight and level through the massed fire of the fleet, emerging unscathed for another run. Economical certainly, but not a good augury for the future. On one occasion in mid-summer we went up to the coast and anchored, with the ship closed down against gas attack. It was unbearably hot down below, while those of us in exposed positions boiled gently under our heavy black oilskins. An aircraft flew over and sprayed us with simulated mustard gas. I am thankful that it was never used against us in reality in that harbour.

Then came our annual inspection by Captain (D), George Creasy. This, of course was vital for Johnny's promotion prospects, competition being friendly but fierce between the four lieutenant commanders' commands in the flotilla. The great day went remarkably well. This was a change from the disastrous inspection I had in China in the *Diana*. At one stage all officers were 'killed' but me, and I had the greatest fun repelling boarders in a haze of explosions and smoke. Later l got a nice write-up in the report: 'I was particularly impressed...etc.' I doubted whether I'd have been as brave with live ammunition. On our return to harbour, Johnny brought her in so skilfully that we had no need of a picking-up rope and we were shackled on to the buoy in a few seconds. I think G. Creasy was impressed.

One of the more entertaining exercises was a simulated landing in Aboukir Bay, the site of Nelson's victory. We crept in at dawn and I landed in charge of a small sabotage party to test the wakefulness of the local militia. On the way in, I looked in the clear waters for signs of Bruey's wrecked fleet, but of course saw nothing. The locals were not alert so we had an enjoyable time commandeering a goods train and shunting it along the line towards Alexandria. Later on we all returned to the beach on short leave with Florrie Foord, his wife and 'sprog'.

Most exercises were a good deal more serious. All through the summer, we were kept busy; busier still when A.B. Cunningham became our most exacting, though human, commander-in-chief. In fact when Johnny got married to Sue Le Gallais, who flew out from England in a large flying boat, their honeymoon only lasted a weekend and off we went to sea again. However, a few weeks later the C-in-C kindly sent us off to Mersa Matruh along the desert coast for a few days' rest. Sue was able to come to stay in the small hotel; she was, as far as I know, the only white lady in the place, it being a restricted military area. We had a good time there swimming in the perfectly clear water where (of course) Cleopatra once swam with Mark Antony. There was a choice of sea or lagoon; both deliciously cool in the hot sun. I got badly burnt and should have known better. We had a jolly beer-drinking time at all levels with the 8th (Royal Irish) Hussars who had recently converted from horses to mechanization and drove around the desert like maniacal steeplechasers. The thinking at the time was that they would run rings round the Italians who only had solid rubber tyres while our people had big inflated balloons which enabled them to go anywhere. To demonstrate this they took some of us for a good run into the desert, which was to be the scene of so much carnage in the next few years. This trip entailed a visit to an Arab sheikh (of sorts) who sat us down on rugs in his tent and had us eat exceedingly dry seedcake washed down (if that is the word) by tiny cups of

Turkish coffee to the tune of a tinny wind-up gramophone. He must have had a sense of humour. I found it almost impossible to swallow my share, but duty had to be done. I think I'd have preferred sheep's eyes.

Then, back to Alexandria and more patrols until it was time for the summer cruise. This took us to Skiathos – then just a little village by the beach, unvisited by tourists. A little 'hydroplaning' behind the 'skimming dish', chasing porpoises who enjoyed the fun. These were the days before water skis. Introduction to Retsina and Ouzo, neither of which appealed. On to Salonika; a plan to visit Sofia just for the hell of it fell through, so the visit turned out to be rather official and dull. On the way south there were more exercises, in one of which we had to close the Fleet flagship *Warspite* in a high wind to pick up mail. Johnny handled the 'Griff' marvellously under the highly critical eye of ABC and got a 'manoeuvre well executed', which pleased us greatly. They didn't come easily.

An anecdote of A.B. Cunningham told to me by Johnny L-B:

> *When Johnny was sub of a destroyer in one of the reserve flotillas based on Port Edgar in the early 1920s, A.B.C. was Captain (D) and lived as a bachelor in the official house just inshore of the destroyer pens. From here he could see everything that went on in the 'boats'. One afternoon, Johnny went ashore in plain clothes and was walking past A.B.C's house when the great man stopped him and asked him which ship he was in and what his duties were.*
>
> > *'The V ...., sir, as navigator.'*
> > *'Have you written the Fair Log up to date?'*
> > *'Not quite up to date yet, sir.'*
> > *'Then go back and do it before you go ashore.'*

I doubt whether anyone normally wrote up the Fair Log every day, but A.B.C. liked to keep people on their toes. He hadn't mellowed much as an admiral twenty years later.

The next item which remains in the memory, was a 'live' bombardment of land targets on Cape Arnautin in Cyprus. I suppose the gunnery was rather primitive compared with later in the war, but one had to keep alert for such signals as 'Adolf and Benito approaching in a bus'. Whereupon we blasted some rocks with satisfactory explosions and great clouds of dust. Afterwards there was a most agreeable visit to Kyrenia where we in the wardroom were plentifully entertained by old Mr. Waring, the furniture merchant, in his villa on the waterfront. A memorable climb up St. Hilarion castle (not to be revisited until 1977) and drinks with a Cypriot – an ardent exponent of Enosis – who owned the circular tower nearby. We had the ship magically illuminate it by searchlight at an appropriate moment after dark. This visit really turned out to be the last of the peacetime Mediterranean. The Fleet would never again dominate the sea and treat the islands as its own. After 150 years this was to be an end, although one was not aware of it at the time.

We left Cyprus and the weather became hot, and so did the international situation. We escorted a dummy convoy from Cyprus to Gaza in torrid heat. My cabin became scarcely bearable with scuttles closed and deadlights down. We had, of course, no refrigerators other than the main meat stowage, or air conditioning of any kind. I kept some water marginally cool by hanging a porous 'chatty' in the airstream from a fan, but it didn't help much. Kenneth Letts was in bad shape with a high fever which had the Flotilla doctor in the *Glowworm* worried. We anchored off Gaza – a miserable strip of dusty palm trees and shacks – and got some fresh air. Then, at last, back to Alexandria where preparations were well under way for the Fleet Regatta and the imminent war.

It was 15 August 1939.

War

At that time, I was still the Confidential Books Officer. In addition to all the regular secret manuals, Fleet instructions and documents, I had to account for various sealed envelopes to be opened only when ordered by the Admiralty. These included our instructions for all the phases leading up to the actual outbreak of war. As far as I can remember, an envelope called 'FUNNEL' put us virtually on a war footing. Warheads were already fitted to torpedoes and shells were fused. Very shortly afterwards our division of four destroyers left Alexandria for Port Said, the Suez Canal and the Red Sea. It was clear that if Italy came into the war, our station was to be in that area, where the Italians had a substantial force of destroyers and submarines of doubtful quality, based on Massawa. This was a dreadfully debilitating place, as I found in 1948 when I was based there for a while, clearing what mines survived from the early war days. Doubtless our task would be the protection of shipping between Aden and Suez. We calculated that we had one round of anti-aircraft shell for each Italian aircraft in the area. But to me it seemed almost worth a war to avoid the Fleet Pulling Regatta, an intensely competitive matter of heavy wooden boats, unwieldy oars, sore backsides and aching arms. It was one of the few forms of exercise that I did not enjoy.

After a quick passage through the canal we found ourselves off Port Sudan when we received the telegram 'TOTAL GERMANY', which meant that the war had started. I was asleep in my bunk at 1400, having kept the middle watch. I remember the messenger waking me with the news which, it seemed to me, could well have waited until I woke up. We were a long way from Germany and there was as yet no sign of Italy becoming involved. Later in the day we went in to Port Sudan to fuel. It was extremely hot. As by now all scuttles and deadlights were closed, my cabin was like a furnace again, and the steel decks were too hot to touch. As we lay alongside, our divisional commander, Cecil Chatwin, walked over to see what we had done about tearing out woodwork and generally making life uncomfortable for war. We had done no such thing and had no intention of doing so. From then on, we were the recipients of a succession of rude signals – possibly justified but regarded by Johnny as 'pinpricks'. Chatwin was a testy little man who wore a monocle. It wasn't long before he ran into trouble himself.

After a rough passage to Aden the division returned to Suez. It was by now clear that Italy was not coming in yet, so we went back up the canal to Alexandria, to find the fleet in, the regatta over, and that no other ships had stripped themselves of wood. So that was one up to us. The next few weeks were spent either in escorting convoys – which had already been organized – or in anti-submarine patrols off Alexandria.

On one of these, the *Garland*, our trying divisional leader came to grief. We had obtained a promising asdic (sonar) contact and were hunting it. The first live depth charge attacks of our war were made, with the usual devastating explosions of water and black foam. At this stage the 'patterns' were dropped fairly shallow at 50 to 250 feet, so one had to steam fast to get clear before they went off. After one such attack *Garland* stopped to investigate results. Unfortunately her last shallow charge had got caught in the rails and had not dropped into the water. While she was still stopped, someone nudged the release lever and down went the charge, to explode close to her stern. The result was fairly spectacular. I saw her stern lift perceptibly and then settle into the water with a marked crinkle in the ship's side abreast the after torpedo tubes.

There seemed to be some danger of her sinking, and we had to take her in tow. We eventually got her into the floating dock in Alexandria harbour just before the worst happened. Luckily there were few injuries as everyone had run like rabbits along the iron deck before the charge went off. This was the first casualty in our flotilla. After many months in dock, *Garland* was turned over to the Polish Navy with her original name. We were to meet her again. Poor Chatwin left his command and vanished from sight. Ironically, it is now certain that there were at the time no German U-boats in the Mediterranean.

Home Waters

After a week or two of escorting convoys, we gradually crept westwards to Gibraltar until about the end of October 1939. Then we left the Mediterranean to take a convoy to England in fairly rough weather. The Mediterranean fleet, probably the most efficient in the navy, was gradually dispersing homewards. This convoy run was without incident. But it gave us practice in station-keeping at night in poor weather without lights. This was, of course, before the days of radar. One relied entirely on eyesight, peering through Barr and Stroud binoculars which as often as not were wet, standing on the open bridge in all weathers. This became quite a strain even in those early days. Although the convoy itself kept a fairly steady course, ships then were not accustomed to station-keeping and tended to stray out of line, bunch up or straggle behind. We had to zigzag back and forth, trying in the dark to make out the dim shapes of the merchant ships, to distinguish the outermost of them and keep an eye on the senior officer. The escort was pitifully thin and we were fortunate that the enemy had not many boats at sea. We still had only three watchkeeping officers apart from Tony Juniper who kept the morning watch. So one usually had four hours on and eight off during which normal shipboard duties had to be performed.

At the end of the run, we were detached to Plymouth, a welcome green sight as always after months in dusty climes. Although not so deserving, I felt as Drake must have felt, making our way up the Sound. Especially welcome it was because we were a Devonport-manned ship, most of the ship's company's families lived in the area and they had been separated for fifteen months. So, a run ashore for each watch as we lay gratefully alongside the dockyard wall awaiting developments.

They were not long in coming. Only a couple of days after our arrival we were hurriedly recalled from leave at midnight and ordered with all despatch to Harwich. The

Germans, so intelligence believed, were about to invade the Low Countries. Such, it seems, had been their plan until weather and other considerations, far beyond our ken, had postponed the operation until the spring. In any case we were needed on the east coast where the German mining campaign was just becoming effective.

It so happened that our flotilla leader, the *Grenville*, was in dock so we embarked Captain George Creasy and his staff and became the temporary leader. G.C. and his staff were a delight to have on board, reflecting his splendid personality. So we accepted the overcrowding and general discomfort with good grace to take our place at the head of the line. On the way up channel we ran into thick fog and began to shiver. It was an abrupt change from the Mediterranean and Red Sea. Also, one had to get used again to strong tides and murky conditions. Early on, I distinguished myself by nearly striking a buoy in the Thames estuary having misjudged the cross current. JLB was understandably sharp, and I learned another quick lesson without mishap.

In the mouth of the Thames were several sad signs of the German mining campaign. There were wrecks of ships with only their upper works standing above the muddy water. It was now early November, time enough to realise that the mines were magnetic, laid on the bottom in shallow water under fifteen fathoms. No effective protection yet existed and there seemed to be no safe way of sweeping them. As all our operations from Harwich were in mineable waters, one never knew, day or night, whether one might be blown up at any moment, so one tended to walk about with knees slightly bent. At one time we were invited to go at full speed through a suspect area, the idea being that a mine might not go off until one was safely past. I never heard of any results either way and was relieved when more sane methods were adopted after Lieutenant Commander Ouvry recovered one of the beasts from the mud at Shoeburyness. Eventually we were degaussed, which made us a good deal less vulnerable.

Harwich turned out to be a fairly agreeable base, although it was quite a trek from the long railway jetty to the Alexandra Hotel, Dovercourt, where we spent a lot of time drinking beer when in harbour. Regrettably, we 'lifted' a large brass ball at the foot of the staircase. This ball became the favourite plaything of Jamie the bull terrier. After a while, a number of flotilla wives turned up, having mysteriously heard where we were. Our seagoing consisted mainly of endless patrols, trying to catch any U-boats which might be laying the mines. Historically, such patrols are known to be fruitless and wasteful of effort. And this proved to be so in our case. Navigation was tricky because of strong tides, variable courses and speeds, few lights and marks, and the existence of our own defensive minefields in some areas. Occasionally this tedious business was lightened by a more aggressive patrol off the Dutch coast, to pickup any German coaster forced out to sea by ice on the canals, or to examine angry Dutchmen inward bound and in sight of home.

Then, the first of many survivors: a ship called *Blackhill* had been mined, but had time to abandon. A few days later, the Italian *La Grazia*. We rescued the crew but weren't sympathetic. Now I felt one great advantage of carrying Captain (D)'s staff. One was no longer alone on the bridge as there was a staff officer to accompany one on watch, help keep a lookout and generally make it easier to stay awake and alert. However, on one occasion I had a tricky moment when the flotilla torpedo officer, much senior to me, was at the compass. We saw a dim red light to starboard. It was on a steady bearing. Obviously we should alter course to give way. Pollard did nothing, so I suggested that she was getting a bit close. 'It's all right,' he said, 'green to green – it's our right of way.' 'But that's a red light.' 'No, green.' The situation was getting both ridiculous and dangerous. Suddenly he realised that collision was imminent regardless of the colour of the light, and took avoiding action. I never discovered whether he was colour blind or had a momentary aberration due to tiredness or sleepiness.

It was about that time that some most welcome additions arrived on board. Some extra crew, and among the officers two sub-lieutenants RNVR – Johnny Blackmore (an equestrian in real life), Clifford ('Button') Studd, and a midshipman RNR, Ian Kenyon. The latter later left the Navy for the RAF, where he was killed. The others became efficient and reliable, and eased the strain a lot. And last, but far from least, Surgeon Lieutenant RNVR Jon Walley, of whom more anon. A remarkable character, a tower of strength in doctoring, singing, drinking and conversation.

When we arrived in Harwich we were honoured to be joined by three Polish destroyers which had escaped the Germans and were avid for revenge: *Burza* of French design, *Blyskawica* (known as the Blistered Vicar) and *Grom* on board which was a namesake of mine who rejoiced in the name of Stratford Hercules Dennis. He later distinguished himself in many ways, ending up as Naval Attaché in Bangkok where he is reputed to have married a Siamese and lived happily ever after. He was appointed liaison officer with the Poles because he could speak Italian (just as the new medical officer at Shotley Boys' Training Establishment was a gynaecologist).

The First Winter

The weather, never very warm in this part of the world, started to get cold early on. I felt physically really miserable at times; soaked with rain or spray on the open bridge; clad in a rather thin duffel coat and clammy rubber sea boots. We had no opportunity to draw much in the way of warm clothing or to buy warm things ashore. My feet were permanently frozen, and I was as seasick as ever. George Creasy, always charming, was persistent and would hunt every asdic echo to the last if there were even the remotest possibility of it being a submarine. In fact we never found one all through that winter, and I have often wondered how many there actually were. But the mines continued to appear and to sink ships, so we had to keep at it. Many had been laid by aircraft, as we were to see. Although I had no inkling of it at the time, German destroyers had made several successful forays into our area at night for this purpose. They had a considerable advantage over us as they were only in our area for a few hours and could be fully alert whereas we were already getting a little weary with constant night watches, peering into the dark through wet binoculars, if only to keep one's fellow destroyers in sight. Luckily for us probably, we never encountered them, although the *Jersey* was badly damaged by their torpedoes off the Humber. My term-mate Norman Macpherson later spent a fair amount of time drying out the pound notes from his safe, which held the pay and was submerged in the ship's office. They turned out to be too oily to use. Everyone thought *Jersey* had been damaged by a mine, such was our preoccupation with them. No one had even seen the enemy. Ironically, *Jersey* was eventually sunk by a mine in the entrance to the Grand Harbour, Malta.

First Losses

In mid-November we were off the Dutch coast rounding up merchant ships when we had our first glimpse of the enemy. Four Dornier 18 flying boats were circling round having a good look at us. They seemed very slow and Johnny suggested to George Creasy that we should go on to thirty knots and ram one. Later that day, one of them was found wrecked in the water. Some survivors were picked up by one of the Poles while their nice rubber raft was taken aboard the *Gipsy*. The survivors were never seen again – the Poles said that they 'perished'.

We all entered harbour that evening. As we arrived there was quite a lot of activity. Some aircraft were being shot at and after we had passed the harbour mouth a Heinkel seaplane was seen to drop a mine on a parachute right in the channel. After we had berthed alongside, a group of us went off to Dovercourt to enjoy the blessings of the land, if not the fruits of our labours. We hadn't been there long when we were abruptly recalled to our ships and ordered to sea. Some German destroyers had been reported off the Dutch coast by the RAF. Great news, except that there was the problem of the mine in the fairway. Captain (D) decided that the risk must be taken, particularly as, if ships kept to the edge of the channel, they might well be clear of the mine.

So off we went, with ourselves leading the line. This time my lifebelt was fully inflated and my knees very bent. As we reached the spot I held my breath but nothing happened. Only a minute later our next astern, the *Gipsy* blew up with an almighty bang and a flash of light. She broke in two right between the funnels. The captain, Nigel Crossley (Uncle Ni-Ni), was catapulted onto the forecastle and never regained consciousness. Robert Franks, also on the bridge, landed on B gun deck in company with the magnetic compass binnacle on which he had been leaning at the time. He was quite unscathed. Johnny Aitken, the sub-lieutenant, got some sailors together, launched the Dornier's rubber dinghy and hardly got wet.

We spent a dismal few hours trying to pick up survivors in the dark with the brown foamy current flowing by and the pervasive smell of oil fuel – later so familiar that it still strikes a chord of memory whenever I smell it. Mingled with the cries of the drowning men was the mournful tolling of the channel bell buoy, a fitting requiem for the first of our flotilla to go. The fore part of the wreck remained visible for years. A sad feature of the evening was the fact that many of the flotilla wives had been watching the ships depart and did not know for some time which was the unlucky one. I suppose that this was the beginning of our feeling that *Griffin* was a lucky ship. And so she turned out to be. It was now that one of our Stoker POs cracked up and went about the ship 'smelling death'. He was put ashore, our first case of what later was called LMF ('Lack of Moral Fibre'). Not nowadays. As a postscript: the four German destroyers turned out to be a false report of ourselves that afternoon.

Indeed it wasn't much later that we were lying alongside the jetty when the *Keith*, trying to make a stern board to shift berth, cut a jagged hole about twenty feet long in our forecastle. There were cries of alarm as the sailors, now quick to react to any untoward noise, abandoned the mess decks like startled birds. The cries turned to cheers – a spell in dock at last, and no one could blame us! So off we went up the Thames for a blissful ten days in the West India docks. Apart from the blackout and the plethora of uniforms, London still seemed to be on a peacetime footing. Food and drink were plentiful, nightclubs full of people and blue smoke. It was irritating to hear them talking about the 'phoney war'. I wished some of them could try a few wet cold nights off the Gabbard, get blown up and go for a swim. Perhaps a lot of them did later.

Ten days was over pretty quickly. Then it was back to Harwich, having lost (D) and his staff who returned to the *Grenville*, now repaired. There was of course a good farewell party at which I remember G.C. singing an excellent French song called *Monsieur de Framboisie*. There was another party at Christmas, which we were lucky to spend in harbour. I remember, emboldened by the drink, doing a female impersonation in a green dress of Sue Lee-Barber's. Next day off to sea again, feeling as green as the dress. This time we were to meet and escort the submarine *Triumph* (Bes McCoy), which had struck a floating mine somewhere off Heligoland. Her bows had been blown off and she was lucky to survive. One of her crew slept all through it in his hammock only a few feet away and was much incensed to be shaken out of his sleep by a survivor. Eventually she made it back into the Medway and we returned to patrol and then Harwich.

Winter Continues

By now the worst winter for many years had set in. It was bitterly cold on the bridge and we still lacked any warm protective clothing. I at least had a reasonably warm cabin to sleep in. I felt for the crew of B gun – always manned – who were very much exposed on watch and then had to try and sleep in the cold damp fug of the mess deck. In Harwich, large ice floes had started to form. These jammed between pairs of ships at the buoys so that sometimes the buoy jumpers could stand on the ice and unshackle before we went to sea.

After New Year's Day we blossomed forth to carry a real live medical officer, Jon Walley, mentioned earlier. He became a lifelong friend. It was also about this time that Robin Rampling and Kenneth Letts left us. Both were feeling the strain and their health broke down. In the Chief's place came Jack Fenn-Clark, a third red beard. When Letts left I took his place as navigator, a job I enjoyed greatly except for the eternal chart correcting and marking of minefields. These were a constant burden when off watch.

Loss of *Grenville*

The exceptionally cold weather had the effect of freezing up many of the German and Dutch waterways, thus forcing much of the water traffic out into the open sea where we could get at it. This meant patrols close off the Dutch coast. The area was by now rather full of mines and to add to one's discomfort, the Dutch shore lights blazed away merrily at night, leaving us exposed to any U-boats to seaward.

On 19 January, the weather had been thick and miserable. We had been out with *Grenville* and *Grenade* for a couple of days, and one or two merchant ships had been sent back to the Downs with boarding parties. In the strong tides, with no visible marks on land, our position was somewhat in doubt. We were steaming in line abreast when *Grenville* blew up amidships and sank rapidly. The water being shallow, her forward and after parts remained for a while above water as the broken sections rested on the bottom. The first thing was to pick up survivors in the water, as they couldn't last long in these temperatures. There were the usual harrowing scenes and sounds with which we were to become so familiar. Her wardroom was lucky – we rescued them all, including George Creasy himself. Cold and wet as he was, he insisted on coming onto the bridge and was only quietened by a 'shot' given him by Jon Walley, which assuredly saved him from death by pneumonia. But only about 100 crew could be picked up. There was one man who somehow found himself outside the forecastle hull, clinging to the bars of the naval store scuttle. For a long time he refused to jump for *Grenade's* boat as he couldn't swim. Later, the *Daily Express* published a remarkable photograph of this. It was thought that there must be others trapped in the still visible fore part. But there was no way of getting at them. Sadly we watched the bows sink.

Our troubles were not over. Remembering the *Aboukir*, *Cressy* and *Hogue* disaster in 1914, we had to bear in mind that there might be a U-boat waiting for another shot. On the other hand, this was probably a mine and if it were a moored mine, we would probably be in the middle of a minefield. I inflated my lifebelt a bit more and bent my knees again. At last we had done all we could, and *Grenade* led us off out of the area. As we left there was another shattering explosion, that time just astern of *Grenade* and ahead of us. Her propeller must have touched a mine. We were both unharmed. Lucky ship, again.

Still none too sure of our position we followed *Grenade* in a snowstorm to anchor just off the coast of England to await the dawn and clearer weather. We were glad to get back to Harwich in one piece and land our survivors. I have since read that the minefield that sank the *Grenville* was laid on 6 January 1940 by the German destroyers *Steinbrinck*, *Eckholdt* and *Ihn*, in position 51.39 N, 02.17 E.

Moray Firth

We had three days in Harwich to recover, and then resumed the usual patrol patterns off Smith's Knoll. We passed a couple more casualties, the Japanese *Terukuni Maru* (no sympathy) and the *Simon Bolivar*. At the end of the month, we were taken in hand for degaussing. This meant the draping of wires all around the hull. When a suitable current was put through the wires, the ship's magnetic 'signature' was reduced to a negligible amount. Theoretically, at least, she was now more or less safe against magnetic mines laid on the seabed. This was certainly a relief although within only a day or two we had a change of scene into deeper waters.

On 2 February 1940, in company with *Gallant*, we patrolled to seaward of a northbound convoy. All was quiet until the evening when a tanker, the *British Councillor* reported being mined or possibly torpedoed. Off at thirty knots to her assistance, we were bothered by an Arado seaplane buzzing about low overhead. The tanker eventually sank. The next evening found us at Rosyth, lying close to a dry dock, which contained the cruiser *Belfast* which had broken her back in a mine explosion, but got safely in. Forty years later, she lies in the river Thames in a state of preservation. It is a pity that no wartime destroyer was thus preserved.

Next day, Johnny Lee-Barber complained of feeling very unwell and was sent off to hospital where he was found, not surprisingly, to have a stomach stoppage. He was told he could not go to sea again, but refused to accept the verdict of the naval doctors and called in a most distinguished Scottish surgeon who, after operating, allowed that further seagoing would be acceptable provided that Johnny gave up drinking gin (before) and port (after) meals. Meanwhile Tony Juniper took temporary command, and a chap called Russell took his place as No. 1, as I was still only a sub-lieutenant. The following day we were patrolling off Aberdeen and Kinnaird Head and then the Moray Firth. The reason for these patrols was the presence of some skilled and rather persistent U-boats. The Admiralty had declared a mined area all along the east coast to seaward of the coastal shipping lane. Its effect, of course, was to cause a 'funnel' at the northern end, through which many ships had to pass, thus presenting a tempting hunting ground for the U-boats. We in turn were to hunt them. So far, they had won the first round, torpedoing the flotilla leader *Exmouth* lost with all hands, and later the *Daring* at the tail end of a Norwegian convoy. We thus spent much sea time on what proved to be rather fruitless patrols, called the Moray Merry-go-round. Several times we thought we were onto a U-boat. On one occasion the *Gallant*, sure of a target, dropped a pattern before it was properly set for depth. Nothing happened. Of course, we were reluctant to steam over that spot in case the charges went off. After a certain amount of signalling, *Gallant* replied, 'I have it on good authority that they will not now explode.' A minute later, they went off, to our intense amusement.

At least we didn't have to worry about magnetic mines, but to make up for this the German air force was busy attacking shipping and light vessels – anything they could find. As we had no radar, nor were there any arrangements for getting warnings from ashore, we had to keep on our toes all the time. Sure enough on 9 March after a jolly night in Aberdeen we were attacked ourselves. A Heinkel 111 came suddenly out of the clouds and ran a stream of machine gun bullets right along our decks from aft to forward. I was on the bridge and was rather narrowly missed by a bullet, which made a nice hole in the deck log, which was lying on the chart table. I kept the log and, as authors say, have it here before me as I write. Sadly we did suffer our first casualty: Cook Shirtleff, in the galley cooking, was hit and died later. A.B. Colley was also hit but only lightly wounded. Considering that the iron deck was full of sailors running to action stations, we were remarkably lucky not to lose more men. The bomb missed, and we hung around for a while trying to 'protect' a nearby merchant ship, though there wasn't much protecting we could do with our inadequate machine guns. We got the merchant ship into Peterhead, landed our casualties and went back to sea.

Most of March was spent at sea around the Moray Firth area. Many depth charges were dropped but nary a U-boat surfaced. The weather was foul but the nights were getting shorter and I think we all felt in better spirits. On entering Invergordon, our base (the scene of the famous mutiny in September 1931, the week I joined the Navy), it is the custom to sound the 'still' as one passes the wreck of the *Natal*, a cruiser which had blown up in 1917 during a children's party. When in harbour we stretched our legs by forming a 'Griffin Wheelers' bicycle team; clad in strange costumes we roamed to moors and took in fresh air and beer.

Then Johnny L-B returned to general congratulations, cured of his stoppage and, officially TT, Jon Walley had to make him drink a filthy 'brown mixture' at regular intervals. It can't have been long before he demanded his first glass of port, and after that he never looked back (in 1995, he still drinks his gin, smokes twenty-five a day and is as much fun as ever at the age of 90). He died in November 1995, having, as he told me, had enough.

On the fairly rare occasions when we were in Invergordon for the night, the shore hospitality was extraordinarily warm, resulting one evening in a splendid party in the wardroom at which Salvatore Sultana ('Salvo', our normally impassive Maltese leading steward) got quite carried away by all the kilts and bagpipes and flung himself into the festivities in a wild Mediterranean dance festooned with table napkins and brandishing a wine salver. This time must have been particularly hard for the Maltese, so far from home. They never complained. Salvo continued to insist that there were only two kinds of fish – Dendici and Lampuki.

Fruitless patrols continued, with the occasional aircraft alarms. On one happy occasion, a Heinkel 111 was despatched into the sea by three Hurricane fighters. We sent a boat over to pick up the pieces. There were no survivors but we recovered some papers and a ship recognition manual. At long last we got a nice break – a boiler clean was long overdue, so we were sent into Dundee for eight blessed days. 'Bonny' was the right word. We were superbly entertained, in particular by the local repertory company, which had some remarkably pretty young ladies. One evening a misguided attempt to drive a dockyard railway engine, which had been left unattended with steam up, could have caused problems had the very Scottish policeman not accepted a large whisky in settlement.

During this brief period leave was given. Most of us took the train south for four days. An incident on the night train shows the state of our nerves. Three of us, including the imperturbable Florrie Foord, were asleep on the benches when for some reason the train rumbled over a rough set of points. There was a shake and a roar. Within seconds, all three of us found ourselves out in the corridor, blowing up imaginary lifebelts. We all felt a bit foolish.

It was good to see some green grass and signs of spring again after so much ice and heather and salt spray. I remember Dick Coulton (a new RNVR sub-lieutenant, and an architect by trade) wondering how many more English springs we'd see. In his case, it was none as he was lost in the *Neptune* the following year in the Mediterranean.

The end of March had us back in the Moray Firth, constantly at sea. The mixture as before: sporadic bombing of small convoys; interminable investigations of contacts, which could be submarines, but never were; constant peering through binoculars, by day for aircraft and by night to keep in station.

Norway

Then, on 3 April 1940, another sudden change of scene. We arrived in Scapa Flow at midnight, filled up with oil and left within the hour for the Clyde. Clearly something was up. No sooner did we arrive in the Clyde than we turned around and headed for Scapa again, arriving on the afternoon of the 6th. I had no wish to stay in that dreary anchorage although many old friends were around, particularly in Gutter Sound, the home of destroyer command. Anyhow, there was no opportunity to get together as we remained at short notice all day, and on the evening of 7 April went to sea with a good force of the Home Fleet – *Rodney* flying the flag of the C-in-C, Admiral Sir Charles Forbes, *Repulse, Valiant, Penelope* and ten destroyers. We were back with a fleet at last, albeit rather an ancient one.

We plunged straight into one of those North Sea gales and pretty soon I was feeling wet, cold and sick. We had little idea of what was happening, but then neither did the commander-in-chief. We know now that we had an expedition ready in the Clyde to occupy certain Norwegian ports if there were any hostile reaction to a mine-laying operation off the Norwegian coast, designed to force German shipping out to sea. For this reason we had gone to the Clyde. But the operation was unfortunately cancelled when the German heavy ships, themselves on the way to Norway, were believed to be trying to break out into the Atlantic. Hence our high speed as we battered off north-eastwards through the night.

Poor Admiral Forbes came in for much criticism – indeed it is said that some called him 'wrong way Charlie'. But the fault lay to a great extent with Winston Churchill himself. Rather irrelevantly, I remembered a little story a friend had told me of a time he was standing in a urinal ashore in Scapa Flow. Alongside him were two figures, one of them dressed for golf. A signals officer came up next to the younger of the two figures, and said, 'Hello, I see you are flag lieutenant now. Which of these silly old B's are you looking after now?' Sir Charles, without looking up, murmured, 'This one.' So he must have had a sense of humour, even though he was a gunnery officer.

To return to sea: next morning we were startled to intercept an emergency signal from our sister ship the *Glowworm* to say she had sighted first one, then a second, German destroyer. *Glowworm* had been with the force covering the mine-laying operation and was 250 miles ahead of us. She reported that she was chasing the enemy. So far, so good. But her next signal reported engaging a nearby ship. Then silence. We did not learn until later that before being sunk she had rammed and damaged the *Hipper* and Gerry Roope, *Glowworm*'s captain, was lost with nearly all the crew. Bobby Ramsay, my opposite number, was picked up and spent the rest of the war as a prisoner. I remember that he had just spent nearly all his last boiler-cleaning leave travelling by train to spend a couple of hours with his current girl friend who lived in Cornwall. He got a DSO, and Gerry Roope, a posthumous VC. So went the third of our flotilla.

The C-in-C detached *Repulse*, *Penelope* and four of the screen to go to the scene but by then the *Hipper* had returned to Trondheim, which, although we didn't know it, was already in German hands. With the rest of the fleet, we continued to batter our way north-eastwards into the gale, but later in the day, turned south. This was a relief from the battering of the sea, but the reason for it was obscure, like the whole situation. In effect we hung about off Bergen all the 9th, quite expecting to be told to go in and assault the port. But it was not to be, and all that happened was a series of air attacks in the afternoon by the new Junkers 88s. Most of their attacks were on the heavy ships, and one bomb hit the *Rodney* without apparent effect. It was good to see the old wagon (she was an old ship of mine) ploughing steadily on without apparent ill effects. But it was infuriating that we had no adequate means of knocking down these aerial pests. If only the Navy had been able to keep its Air Arm after the First War.

At one stage the *Gurkha* had turned down wind to get a steadier gun platform – her captain being a distinguished gunnery officer. All that was achieved was to separate her from the main body, resulting in her being sunk later in the day. The lesson that we should stick together in the face of air attack was one that we thus learned early. But one saw it ignored later in the war, always with sad results.

It was on this occasion that we first encountered the use of radar (called RDF in those days). The flagship regularly gave good warning of each new wave of air attack. I could not imagine how aircraft could be spotted so far away.

One suggestion was that they were reported by radio from Norway, but the real reason soon became known. At least one had some warning when in company with properly fitted ships. Otherwise it was binoculars and sharp eyes, such as A.B. Morgan who often saw them first and would deliver his reports in a maddeningly slow, steady tone of voice, showing no emotion whatever. The total enemy force was counted as 47 Ju.88s and 41 He 111s and not one of them was shot down.

The following day we were detached to Sullom Voe in the Shetlands for fuel. We passed a pleasant day there on the 11th, little knowing that the *Scharnhorst* and *Gneisenau* were passing to the south of us only forty miles away. On the evening of the 12th we left the Voe in pitch dark, feeling our way past the boom defences, which were only tiny black blobs of buoys holding up the nets. Next morning we joined Troop Convoy NP1, an impressive array of liners including the *Reina del Pacifico, Duchess of Bedford, Empress of Australia* (I was to take passage in her years later – 1950 – from Malta to Liverpool; by then she was little more than a rust heap), *Monarch of Bermuda, Batory* (Polish), and *Chrobry*. The escort was formidable too: the battleship *Valiant*, cruisers *Manchester, Birmingham, Cairo* and *Vindictive*, and ten destroyers. The Admiralty did not intend to lose any soldiers at sea.

On passage, there was only one U-boat scare when an otherwise unaccounted-for explosion occurred. We now know that the U-boats were having trouble with the magnetic pistols on their torpedoes, so it seems likely that this one went off prematurely. We hadn't time to stay and hunt, so found nothing. However, later that day the *Fearless* and *Brazen* sank U-49 in the entrance to Andfiord, which we all entered a little later. The force, originally intended for an assault on Narvik, could not land there directly because the Germans now held it. So we spent some time shepherding the liners into the fiord at Harstad and then patrolling round them while the military started to set up a base. It was while we were doing this that the cruiser *Aurora* came steaming by at high speed, flying the Union Flag at her fore – the flag of an admiral of the fleet at sea (I believe this was the only time I have seen such a rarity). It was no less a person than Admiral of the Fleet the Earl of Cork and Orrery, that same Ginger Boyle who had lectured to us a couple of years earlier on 'the offensive spirit'. We made a signal to the destroyer: 'Where's the fire?' The reply came at once: 'In *Aurora*'. And very appropriate it was too. Lord Cork wanted to attack at once, but the military wouldn't agree. It was another example of the shambles of the whole campaign. In *Griffin*, our spirits were still high, and it was champagne on the bridge to celebrate Johnny's birthday in the crisp clear air among all those snowy mountains and dark waters.

Next day it was back with the *Valiant* to Scapa where we passed the sad sight of my old ship, the *Suffolk* limping in with her quarterdeck awash. She had been told to bombard the German-held airfield at Stavanger, only to disturb that nest of Junkers 87 dive bombers – at that time, an unknown quantity though not for long. We had a nice three-day rest in Scapa but then left at 25 knots for Rosyth, arriving on the evening of the 22nd. Next day was occupied in embarking a battalion of the Green Howards (Colonel Stansfield), and early on the 24th we set off on Operation Sickle – a landing at Aandalsnes. With us were three cruisers, *Manchester*, *Birmingham* and *York*. At 8 pm we were off Molde, where some of the troops were landed, including some Royal Marines. It was a relief to get into the fiords as the weather continued to be filthy and many of the soldiers were seasick. A few Norwegian fishing boats lay around. Some waved but others seemed to pretend that we weren't there. In the half-light of the late evening we went alongside in Aandalsnes, a pretty little fishing town with wooden buildings crowding down to the water. The soldiers went off on their mission, and we heard they were in action only six hours later. The Germans were getting rather close. Then a lone bi-plane Gladiator fighter flew low overhead – the first and only friendly aircraft with the whole campaign. He was shot down in short order and from then on all aircraft were hostile.

It wasn't long before Aandalsnes was in flames. After landing stores and ferrying some wounded out to the cruisers, we left at 4 am, having had no sleep. It was obvious that the military landing was going to be a forlorn hope. We were sorry for the 'pongoes' who had little of the necessary equipment. I remember one signals officer, heavily laden with a big box of whiskers sticking out of it, being asked what it was for. 'Haven't a clue old boy,' he replied cheerfully through a big ginger moustache.

Polares

A t last, clear of the land, I went to my bunk to snatch a little rest. But only an hour or two later, at I0.45, I was hurriedly shaken and told to get ready to board. I was, I suppose, the boarding officer, though I hadn't given much thought to the implications in our present circumstances. On arrival on the bridge I was quickly briefed. An hour or so earlier, the destroyer *Arrow* had reported that she had approached an apparently neutral fishing trawler, which had suddenly turned and fired two torpedoes at her. *Arrow* had blown her out of the water and her report of the incident arrived just as our bridge had sighted a trawler marked with a big painted Dutch flag, steaming northwards. Clearly this could be another such tartar, and I was to board her to find out.

Johnny manoeuvred the ship bows onto the trawler clear of any likely line of torpedo fire. I hastened into the whaler with Johnny Blackmore, Ian Kenyon and half a dozen sailors including PO Barry and Signalman Brown. The weather was still foul. The sea was rather rough, only just fit for boat work. We had only about half a cable to pull over (regatta, at last?), and as we approached her it became obvious that a 'boat' abaft her funnel was nothing more than a canvas mock-up. Moreover, she seemed to have a lot more men on deck than one would expect for a trawler on passage. There wasn't time to feel more than normally frightened, and in only a minute or two we were alongside, heaving up and down in the swell. Johnny Blackmore and I leaped on board, to be confronted by a slightly dazed looking individual who at once announced the words: 'German ship!' Indeed, so she was: *Schiff 26*, alias *Polares*, alias YP 2623 (her peacetime name had been *Julius Pickenpack*). Very interesting she looked. The canvas mock-up covered a gun, and right away I could see her two torpedo tubes, barely covered by fishing nets. Leaving two boat keepers in the whaler, the rest of my boarding party scrambled aboard, and we quickly got all the German crew on deck. We brandished our loaded .45 pistols just like in the movies. They didn't give any trouble, I believe for two main reasons: they had never expected to be boarded in such weather, and anyhow felt that their disguise was sufficient. There was an acrimonious argument between the original fishing crew and the naval party who had taken over, and the German army passengers, about what should be done.

In the event they didn't resist but threw overboard all their confidential books, cyphers and charts. The books did not sink at once and were recovered very gallantly by Florrie Foord who dived from *Griffin*'s quarterdeck into the rough sea. In doing so, he was not far off drowning but was successfully hauled back on board with his bag of books. He later got the MBE for this effort, a distinction which we felt to be inadequate (Florrie had dived overboard on another occasion before the war when, at a party, a lady's hat had blown over the side. Quick as a flash, Florrie jumped in and retrieved it.)

Meanwhile we were getting busy on board *Polares*. I put Kenyon on the bridge where he succeeded in stumbling and letting off his pistol. Although clumsy, this had a good effect in that it cowed the Germans in the well deck who could not see what had happened. I went around the ship to make sure they were all up top and that she was not being scuttled. While I was doing so one of the crew approached me and warned me in English that the after-hatch leading to the magazine was booby-trapped. After a bit of thought I decided to leave it well alone, and started to ship some of the German crew over to the *Griffin*, leaving enough on board to steam her – she was coal-burning and required quite a bit of stoking.

The naval officer in command turned out to be a Lieutenant Heinz Engelein. He took me to his cabin, asking to get his cap and presented me with his binoculars and the ship's badge – of his last ship, the destroyer, *Erich Giese* (she was the destroyer which torpedoed the *Jersey* on 9 December; she was later sunk at Narvik). I also disposed of the trawler skipper and all the German army people who looked to be a more dangerous lot than the sailors. In exchange, we took on a few more sailors from *Griffin*, as it was clear that I had a good chance of getting *Polares* home.

At this moment, Johnny L-B signalled that he must leave us on our own as *Griffin* had been ordered to go with all despatch to the assistance of the *Flamingo*, which had been bombed. So, feeling a little lonely, I shaped course for home. This was not all that easy, as our initial position was uncertain and I soon discovered that all the charts and navigational equipment had gone overboard. However, we found a small herring fishery chart – a relic of peacetime – and were able to figure out a rough course to steer. I reckoned that we should make for the Shetland Islands to the south-westward, a fairly wide target.

Off we went with Johnny Blackmore and me on the bridge, a German helmsman and a Stoker PO in the boiler room, and a number of German stokers who seemed willing enough. We were outnumbered but kept alert and stuck close to our weapons. The trip home was great fun. A big fat Bavarian chef cooked us some huge meals of bacon and eggs – *Polares* had just come from Denmark. We painted out the Dutch insignia and couldn't resist flying the white ensign over the swastika, although I suppose this might have given the game away to a U-boat.

The ship had some interesting equipment; her cargo was recorded by the Admiralty later as:

  2 torpedo tubes with torpedoes
  4 magnetic mines
  2 field guns
  1 concealed gun
  1 anti-aircraft machine gun
  Depth charges
  A 'mountain of explosive stores'
  'She constitutes a regular arsenal'

She was also fitted with a rather elementary hydrophone. There were papers and operation orders all over the place. These we tried to collect and set aside for the intelligence people. It took two days to reach Scapa Flow. We sighted Muckle Flugga in the Shetlands, which was lucky as visibility was very low and I was anxious about outlying rocks. Then we turned south for the night, to turn west again at dawn, hoping to decry the Orkneys. West we steamed, on and on. No land in sight. I began to wonder whether we were heading out into the Atlantic. Then 'Sparks' got the radio going, and a D/F bearing put us well south of Wick. The German stokers had shovelled so hard that we had made a good deal more southwards than we'd estimated. Just at this moment, cliffs appeared ahead out of the murk and we ran into a heavy cross swell off the land. The ship took a list and stayed over to starboard. I thought the Germans might have chosen this moment to scuttle the ship so we herded them all on deck and had a good search below. It turned out that the coal in the bunkers had shifted, so we had them shovelling hard until she was on an even keel.

From then on all was easy and I made what I felt was a triumphant entry into Scapa Flow, taking care to pass close to the flagship, then at Sunday divisions. As nobody had told me where to go, I made for Gutter Sound where I found that *Griffin* had got in before us, so I went alongside her. Before disembarking, I allowed my sailors to help themselves to the remains of the Danish food and supplies, plus a souvenir German sailor's cap, having made sure that nothing of importance was taken. It was while we were transferring ourselves back to the *Griffin* that an old dugout commander arrived on board to take over my prize. Almost as soon as we got on the bridge, he helped himself to the barometer. It was this gentleman who, in his report, accused us of looting the ship, resulting in a letter expressing Their Lordship's displeasure and eventually in my having to turn in my binoculars, which I still regard as a legitimate prize of war. I had warned Commander 'Dugout' that the mechanism for putting the engines astern was faulty – a piece of advice he scorned from one so green. So I was delighted when he parted the cable on anchoring, having failed to take the way off.

Much later I did get a mention in despatches, but otherwise heard no more until long after the war when I read an interesting mention of the affair in the official history: *British Intelligence in the Second World War* by F.H. Hinsley, et al. The capture is mentioned, with the remark that 'insufficient attention was paid to capturing codes and cyphers', including the Enigma machine. They do not seem to have realized that all this (except for some Enigma wheels, which enabled our cryptographers to decipher several weeks' messages) was thrown overboard before I boarded (and some books recovered by Florrie Foord). The incident is also mentioned in *Alan Turing: The Enigma* by Andrew Hodges, concerning 'Patrol Boat VP 2623' from Germany to Narvik. As an instance of how history is sometimes distorted, I recently found an Admiralty file in the Public Records Office at Kew, in which the capture was attributed to HMS *Repulse*, a battle cruiser then at Scapa Flow. The file concerned an argument about a movie film, which had been taken by a publicity crew who were in Scapa at the time. The film showed *Polares* coming alongside *Griffin* and German sailors being transferred as prisoners. The argument was about whether this film should get publicity as propaganda. It was decided that it should not, as it was hoped to keep the capture secret. Even in some post-war reference books, *Polares* is shown as 'mined'.

A final postscript to this little adventure. In the old days 'prize money' was shared among those who made the capture, including the senior officer responsible, so that some people did very well out of it. It was just my luck that after the Second World War, in the interests of so-called 'fairness', all prize money was put into a central fund and divided among the whole Navy, including, no doubt, a lot of people who had never seen a shot fired.

Long after this was written, the relevant documents have been declassified and an excellent book on the subject of Enigma has been written by Hugh Sebag-Montefiore (*Enigma: the Battle for the Code*). It includes a description of this incident. He 'interviewed' me on the telephone several times, mostly at 2 am (my time).

Namsos

I would have liked some rest and sleep after these enjoyable but tense days. But it was off to sea again the following evening to meet a troop convoy which was to evacuate the army from Namsos after another disastrous retreat. The convoy consisted of some quite large, fast French troopships from the North African run, with excellent Arab names: *El Djezair, El Mansour, El Kantara, El Djebel*. There was a strong escort including the cruisers *Devonshire* (Admiral John Cunningham), *York, Carlisle* and the French *Montcalm*. The destroyers were *Kelly* (Mountbatten – our first contact with him in this war), *Afridi, Nubian, Maori, Hasty, Imperial, Grenade* and ourselves.

On 2 May we found ourselves off Namsos, but there was thick fog at a low level. Four of us were detached to try to find our way into the harbour and embark the soldiers. In some ways the fog should have been a relief, as it should have shielded us from air attack. But it didn't work out that way because our masts were showing above the fog while the German aircraft were in clear weather overhead. There ensued some unpleasant moments while we manoeuvred at high speed with the enemy buzzing overhead dropping bombs on what he could see of us. *Maori* was nearly hit and suffered some casualties while the rest of us were lucky not to have collisions in the confusion. However, no further damage was done and as darkness came on we felt our way up the fiord behind *Kelly* who did some masterly navigation under difficult conditions.

As luck would have it, the fog lifted just at the wrong time to reveal a scene of fire and destruction. Namsos was in flames and so were some trawlers which had been in the fiord all day. Jon Walley was landed alone to cope with the wounded survivors of *Gaul* and *Arab* and had an exciting time with forty-eight of them in a shallow cave, shooting from time to time at passing aircraft. The skipper of one of the trawlers – *Stannard* – later got a Victoria Cross for his efforts. I didn't see much of the evacuation itself as I got my head down for an hour or so, being completely exhausted and without sleep for a couple of days. But we managed to take on our quota of soldiers, British, French and Norwegian, and to re-embark our own people without loss. I re-awoke as we left the town, burning furiously. An old friend, Bill Blake, the naval officer in charge, was lost here.

The convoy was formed up outside the fiord, and we hastened to join them to get some protection from their more powerful anti-aircraft fire. By daylight we were well clear of the fiord and headed home at fifteen knots. Then started a day of bombing attacks by Junkers 87s – our first acquaintance with Stukas. They were a formidable foe, well trained and brave. They seemed to leave the main convoy fairly well alone to concentrate on the destroyers on the screen. The first casualty was a large French destroyer, the *Bison*, which sank after a heavy explosion. Her surviving crew and load of soldiers were picked up by the *Afridi* and *Grenade* while the convoy steamed on.

The next wave of Stukas, having returned to their base and bombed up again, concentrated on these two. This time it was the *Afridi* which was hit by a bomb, which fell just forward of B gun and started a serious fire. To our consternation *Imperial* and we were detailed to stay and help. Obviously this meant that we would be the targets of the next attack which could be expected in a couple of hours. *Afridi* looked in poor shape and Johnny decided to go alongside. It was a dramatic moment. The Captain of the *Afridi*, Philip Vian (known to us, I regret to say, as the 'dead horse', and later to become famous) stood on the bridge, quite unmoved amid a fog of smoke and exploding ready-use ammunition. 'Take me in tow, Lee-Barber.' Well, we couldn't refuse, but the prospects looked dim. As we lay alongside the fires got worse. It seemed unlikely that she would survive to be towed. Also I had an uncomfortable feeling that her forward magazine might be about to explode, taking us all with it. To make matters worse, many of her people were trapped in her forward mess decks by the fire. They opened the scuttles forward and were crying for help but the openings were too small for them to get out. It was a sickening situation, especially as she was gradually going down by the bows, and although they could be touched there was nothing we could do to save them (as a result of this experience, we all later had 'escape scuttles' fitted, big enough for a man to slip through. It is surprising that such a need had not been noted before).

It was not long before Vian had to accept the inevitable and abandon ship. He went over to the *Imperial*, by now alongside *Afridi's* other side. Between us, we took off all the remaining survivors, a shattered mixture of British and French sailors, Chasseurs Alpins, British soldiers and Norwegians, many of whom had by now been sunk twice on top of all their other tribulations. They had no desire to go below but had to be made to go, or we would have turned over with all that top-weight. We watched *Afridi* sink bows first, carrying those wretched men in the forecastle with her. As she dived vertically downwards, *Imperial* and we worked up to full speed to rejoin the convoy and comparative safety.

We reckoned we had about half an hour before the next wave. Sure enough, about that time, back they came. They seemed to work in threes, circling rather arrogantly in the sun before diving one after another at an almost vertical angle, flattening out at a little over masthead height (or so it seemed). They had 'screamers' fitted to instil terror, making a hideous noise as they dived. Johnny avoided all nine with great skill, turning as far as possible into the dive at thirty knots. With all the extra weight on board, this meant a rather sickening rollover at each turn, and one wondered while watching the bombs (one large, four small) whether we might not turn right over anyhow. Our miserable .5″ machine guns were quite useless, and our 4.7″ guns would not elevate to such angles. So the Stukas had virtually no opposition. Of course there were no friendly aircraft within hundreds of miles.

Well, as it turned out, neither ship was hit this time. Lucky 'Griff', once again – or was it skill? The important thing was to see the aircraft in the sun, and we'd got pretty sharp at that. 'Where...where?' Johnny would say, and once he had spotted it, one felt better. Anyhow all was well, apart from some not unnatural panic among the soldiery.

At last we were out of range and were detached to Sullom Voe in the Shetlands, where there lay a French hospital ship. Until then Jon Walley had his work cut out with the many burned and wounded. A story went round, possibly apocryphal, of his slinging an amputated foot out of the sickbay scuttle, narrowly missing a startled sailor. To our chagrin, the hospital ship would take only Frenchmen, making one wonder about this alliance. So it was on to Scapa Flow with the rest, and a day or so to clean up and rest.

Next day we were at sea again escorting the *Warspite* to Greenock. A perfectly lovely peaceful day down the Minches made a contrast with the previous mayhem. At Greenock we fuelled alongside the *Kelly*. While disconnecting the hoses, some of our oil splashed over the *Kelly*'s side. She was already a good deal sprucer than we were, having recently come out of dock after a collision. She seemed to us to have spent a good deal of time in dock for one reason or another. However, an apology was called for to the Lord (Mountbatten). It wasn't long before *Kelly* stopped a torpedo from an E-boat off the Dutch coast and was covered with oil all over. We had a bit of a laugh over that.

We had one night in Greenock but were too exhausted to think of going ashore. It was just as well that we got some sleep, as next day we were ordered to proceed to Dover with all despatch. It was 10 May 1940 and Hitler had at last invaded Holland, Belgium and France.

Holland

There was one immediate personal problem. I was navigator, and one of my jobs was to make sure that all minefields and dangerous areas were entered on the charts. During the Norwegian campaign I had had no time or inclination to enter all the changing information, which constantly flowed in concerning the west and south coasts and lower North Sea. So, as we plunged south, I was fully occupied in just keeping ahead of our progress. Next day we arrived at Dover, completed with oil, and sailed at once for the Dutch coast with *Venomous* and *Codrington*, the latter now commanded by George Creasy, our Captain (D).

The news from Holland was already bad, and we were at action stations as soon as we left Dover. By now, I was rather frightened as well as tired. We'd had a fair taste of unopposed air attack and obviously there was going to be plenty more of that. As the flat Dutch coast came in sight, I found myself losing a bit of bladder control, both uncomfortable and embarrassing.

We were soon off the Hook where we could see on the beaches the empty gliders from which the Germans had landed. A huge pall of smoke marked the destruction of

Rotterdam. German air activity, luckily, was concentrated on land targets but the occasional bomber (Ju.88) kept us alert and busy. The weather was lovely with brilliant sunshine and occasional clouds. By now, one searched the sky with the greatest attention. The lookouts kept reporting the planet Venus, high in the sky, as an aircraft, even at noon.

Our first instructions were to patrol off Ijmuiden and 'shoot at the paratroopers'. This wasn't much use as they were already inland. Very soon, however, *Codrington* went in to evacuate the Dutch Royal family and a load of gold, while we provided cover to seaward. While so engaged we received an alarming signal direct from the Admiralty – an unusual procedure for a humble destroyer.[6] We were directed to go to the Dutch naval base at Den Helder to help the Dutch army by bombarding the dam across the mouth of the Zuyder Zee, along which the German army were said to be crossing. A further signal read ominously, 'If ship is sunk or grounded, take all measures to destroy confidential material.'

With this comforting thought in mind, we steamed along the coast. By now, the weather had become hazy, and it was hard to distinguish much on shore. As we approached the port, we saw a ship ahead. Within a minute, she opened fire on us. However, we soon identified her as the Dutch *Jan van Brakel*, and ourselves to her as friendly, so shortly afterwards a Dutch pilot came out and up onto our bridge. He was drunk and very excitable. As we went up the channel, the lookout reported a mine floating not far from our track. 'Mine! Full speed!' yelled the pilot down the voicepipe. A few minutes later about nine Messerschmitt 110 fighters appeared. 'Dutch?' he cried hopefully. 'No,' we said. 'Britisch?' 'No, sorry German.' 'Ach! Der Boggers! Schoot at dem!' No fear – we wanted to remain as inconspicuous as possible. The Me 110s swept on to strafe the airfield on Texel Island with great efficiency. Luckily, we were not in the game plan.

On arrival off Den Helder naval base, Johnny had to go ashore, leaving Tony Juniper in charge. We lay uncomfortably stopped, awaiting another air attack. Nothing much happened and after a while Johnny returned. The Dutch Admiral had emphatically denied that any help was needed. There appeared to be rather a lot of drunkenness and a strange air of negligence. After duly informing the Admiralty, we were recalled to Harwich, leaving thankfully at dusk to be gently sprayed by machine gun bullets from a passing aircraft, which might well have been British.

After fuelling again at Harwich, with only a short rest, we were again sent to Den Helder where the situation was said to be deteriorating. This time we approached in the dark. We were met by a motor launch, which invited us to follow it through the minefield. However, we now had on board a Dutch naval officer who became suspicious of the inhabitants of the launch. He advised delay, and proved to be right. We soon found out that Den Helder was in German hands, having surrendered while we were away. The launch would doubtless have led us to perdition. Lucky again!

Leave

After some delay reporting the situation, we were again ordered back to Harwich where we arrived on the morning of 15 May. It had been a busy week. After a blissful night's rest we went up to Immingham on the Humber to escort the old submarine depot ship *Cyclops*. While we were there came the joyful news that we were to do a short refit at our homeport, Devonport. It was indeed about time, as we were beginning to show signs of wear and tear having been continuously at sea since the war began; and, indeed for some time before that. So we had nearly four weeks break at a time when all hell was loose in France. I went to my parents in Cheshire for most of my ten days' leave. I also spent a few days with one of my aunts at Bramley in glorious weather, revelling in being alive and on shore, rather oblivious of Dunkirk and other disasters. Somehow one didn't expect anything else. Although in some ways it was a pity to be out of it, we were probably lucky to miss that evacuation (we'd get plenty more later). Two more of our flotilla were lost during it. *Grenade* got a bomb down her funnel while alongside in Dunkirk harbour (my friend Bremer Horne got away dry-shod); and *Grafton* was torpedoed by E-boats just off the beaches. Now there were three of us left undamaged or afloat out of the original nine.

France

Refit over, it was off to sea again on 14 June to our new station, Dover. It promised to be an interesting situation as the Germans were by now established in Calais. After an uneventful patrol, we escorted the cruiser *Galatea* to Portsmouth, anchoring in the morning at Spithead to await developments. While lying there, the news came of the surrender of France. Like a lot of people in England we felt a certain sense of relief that we were on our own. One did not feel that the war was lost and certainly Churchill's radio broadcasts had a most stimulating effect. At the back of my mind lurked the feeling that we were a lucky ship and, if the worst came to the worst, would be one of those to continue the fight from Canada. Meanwhile there was a tough time ahead. Next day we were off to Plymouth again and on to St. Nazaire with the object of embarking the Polish division, which had retired there in good order.

The run down there was fascinating. All kinds of debris from the French debacle were to be seen: huge palls of smoke over Brest; all manner of small craft carrying fleeing refugees; a lifeboat full of Frenchmen; *Viscount* towing the old Duke of Westminster's yacht *Cutty Sark* and the French destroyer *Ouragan* being towed over to Plymouth. The story went that when the Navy took over, the captain pressed a button in his day cabin and found the engineer in his bunk via a moveable partition. Unlikely but fun.

To add to the entertainment, we were wrestling with a kite. During our refit, we had some slight improvements made to our anti-aircraft capability – hitherto virtually non-existent. One set of torpedo tubes had been sacrificed to make way for an antiquated 3" anti-aircraft piece. It was most unlikely to hit anything but might deter the chicken-hearted, of whom there were not many in those days. We had also been supplied with a winch, a great length of piano wire on a reel, a pulley at the top of the mainmast, and a big white kite. The idea, born, I think, of desperation, was that the kite should be flown at the sort of height at which the Ju.87 dive-bomber let go his bombs, thus putting him off his stroke. There was even talk of putting up a lethal device such as a hand grenade on it, but we wisely thought that it would be more likely to damage ourselves. Later, in Alexandria, it was suggested that a pseudo-lethal device would serve the purpose provided the enemy got to hear of it through the flourishing spy route.

And so one ship fitted their kite with a French letter full of treacle, which is reputed (apocryphally, I'm sure) to have fallen into an admiral's barge when the wind dropped. Anyhow, our kite raised problems of its own. When zigzagging, it took on a personality: straight up and steady on one course; down to the sea going with the wind and, in between, circling madly around the masthead, threatening to decapitate anyone in its path. After a while, it fell into the sea. We were unprotected but easier in our minds.

We arrived off St. Nazaire early in the morning, uncertain of our reception by the French, to say nothing of the Germans who were by now in Nantes only fifty miles away. Getting into the lock was tricky as the tide was ebbing fast at right angles to the entrance. However, we got in after a certain amount of manoeuvring at full speed; we certainly didn't want to damage ourselves or run aground at this point. On arrival alongside there was to be seen a motley crowd of people, none in the least like soldiers. They turned out mainly to be Spanish refugees from General Franco, desperate to get out before the Germans arrived. Sadly, we had to turn them down. It soon became apparent that the French would not allow the Poles into the town for fear of air attack and other reprisals. One could feel the general air of defeat and hopelessness. But after a while it was learned that the Poles were on a beach not far away, so without delay we got out and searched up the coast. So far, no air attack although one expected it at any moment.

After a couple of hours steaming, we found them at La Baule. There they were, a whole division of soldiers in dusty khaki, wearing unusual caps. They came out in fishing boats, as we lay off the beach, as close in as possible. There was some competition between us and the next destroyer for one of the leading boats, which was observed to have a couple of good-looking uniformed girls on board. We got them and were impressed to find that they carried evil-looking Tommy guns, apparently well used. It was a perfect day for lying off the beaches except for the constant worry of impending air attack, so one was anxious to get away. In fact, the loading was rapid and orderly and it wasn't long before we had embarked all we could carry. A little after 1 pm we were off again at twenty-five knots, leaning over rather heavily at each turn of the zigzag.

There were some magnificent figures among the Poles. I particularly remember one colonel, fitted with a splendid sweeping moustache, a man from the Napoleonic age. He remained standing on the quarterdeck all day and all night until we reached Plymouth. It was not to be the last time (or the first) that I was impressed by the Polish spirit. In the evening there was a diversion to pick up the survivors of a French tanker, the *Brumaire* (a revolutionary name from a decadent age), which had just been sunk by bombs. Miraculously, it seemed, we were not menaced at all, in which we were lucky as within hours the troopship *Lancastria* was sunk at St. Nazaire with heavy loss of life.

Next morning saw us back at Plymouth, to hand over our soldiers and a few miscellaneous refugees to be processed. My navigator's notebook reads, 'End of a perfect trip. Thank God.'

Interlude

Time, after fuelling, for two hours sleep and then to sea again, this time to escort the new aircraft carrier *Illustrious* on the first leg of her trip to Bermuda to work up. We were envious at the time, but perhaps better off in the long run. The only incident that I remember at all vividly happened the following dawn. I had the morning watch with Midshipman Kenyon. We were keeping station on the carrier in the dark zigzagging at about twenty knots. Having no radar, one relied on binoculars and one's judgement of the distance of a somewhat dim, dark shape. For a minute or two I dozed off and when I came to, I searched for the 'shape' and couldn't find it. I soon saw that Kenyon had been as unconscious as I had been. A quick horrified calculation told me that we had missed a 'zig' inwards (luckily it wasn't outwards). So I piled on some revs and hoped to close her again. No sign. Then the sky became lighter with the early dawn, and I saw *Illustrious*' mast on the horizon, greatly relieved but appalled at its distance. I managed to close a bit before Johnny came up at dawn, but had to admit my error. The rest of the watch passed rather coolly.

PART II

The Finest Hour

Straits of Dover

Back, then, to Plymouth for a day's rest and then to our original station at Dover. It was now 28 June 1940. Dover was, of course, about as near the front line as the surface Navy could get, and it was an interesting experience. As yet fairly undamaged, life seemed to go on ashore much as usual, especially in the yacht clubs and bars. The barmaids seemed a good deal more unmoved than we were by the presence of the German army twenty-odd miles away. Invasion seemed very likely, and the receipt of intelligence reports showing aerial photographs of massed barges in the continental waterways gave notice that something was being prepared.

Our job was partly to cover the brave coastal convoys, which were still operating through the Straits, and partly to be the first warning – particularly at night – of any sea-borne threat. So we settled in to a pattern known as the Prostitute's Patrol – out every night and, when our turn came around, out by day as well. The day patrol meant almost certain air attack and it was hard to distinguish friend from foe; for the first time in our experience some of the aircraft could be, and often were, friendly. It was good to see a Dornier 17 glide slap into the sea, bounce a few times, then sink. The pilot, who survived, was arrogant and insisted that he wouldn't be a prisoner for long. He was told that Canada was a long way off.

At night we patrolled between the Downs and Beachy Head. There was always plenty going on. Naturally we were a little bit edgy. Any object to seaward could be the advance guard of the invasion, although it was early days yet. Being 'watch and watch' when not at action stations meant that one got little sleep, so on return to Dover one tended merely to eat and sleep. On one occasion, at dawn, we actually received a report of an enemy, which turned out to be a shore lookout's report of ourselves. On another occasion, a type of rocket gun at Dover fired off at a German aircraft, releasing a string of small parachutes, designed for the aircraft to run into. These were reported as parachutists and we were hauled out of our well-earned slumber for a false alert.

On the evening of 6 July we endured our heaviest air attack yet. Thirty-six Dorniers made straight for us, in four formations of nine each. As we were the lone destroyer on patrol, there was no one else for them to attack. However, we had plenty of time as they approached slowly at a steady height. Johnny weaved her around at high speed, and the first three groups missed satisfactorily. But the last one didn't. With the ship swinging at thirty knots, I remember lying on the deck of the bridge as a torrent of bombs came straight down on us. There was an almighty series of explosions in the water all round. The ship jumped as though she had a huge hiccup. Then a drenching shower of dirty black water through which we steamed gaily without a scratch, apart from some leaks down below. We entered harbour – only a few miles away – to survey the cause of the leaks, which were not serious. So within half an hour we were off to chase some E-boats, without success.

So it went on, exciting but exhausting for a couple of weeks. Our next solitary patrol on Sunday the 14th (we always seemed to get Sundays) had us covering a convoy off the Downs. We were all heavily attacked again by Heinkel 111s and had to go to the assistance of a small steamer called the *Balder* which had been hit aft and was on fire. We went alongside and managed to put the fire out with hoses. All the while there lay in her well deck a dead man, stark naked, having had all his clothes blown off by the blast. Otherwise, he looked quite uninjured but had an aggrieved expression as though someone had interrupted his sleep. In addition, her deck was littered with hand grenades. She had evidently been fitted with one of those devices of desperation – a pipe pointing upwards with steam led to it by a pin-valve. The idea was that when the aircraft dived on you, you pointed the pipe at it and dropped a hand grenade in. The grenade hit the pin, let off the steam, which then spat the lethal ball at the aircraft. We were told that the grenade would sometimes stick in the pipe, and less intelligent but aggressive people would poke at it with a broom handle. Anyhow, not long after this incident with the *Balder*, Tony Juniper found several grenades on our mess decks, some equally unintelligent sailors having taken them as souvenirs. We got the *Balder* going, towing her alongside, and eventually turned her over to a proper tug, the *Lady Brassey*, who took her into Dover while we remained on patrol.

This time we had the pleasure of being outside while Dover harbour was bombed. But we didn't laugh long because on Friday the 19th it was our turn to be in harbour when the same thing happened. This time it was ten Ju.87s as I could well recognise from the noise. We had just finished lunch, and Johnny's father was on board as a guest (he must have been crazy). I was in my cabin about to go to sleep when the alarm bells went and almost immediately afterwards, the familiar scream of bombs. I lay on the deck, face inboard, to find my face a couple of feet from old Richard Lee-Barber who actually looked as though he was enjoying himself. I wasn't.

Once again, the whole ship seemed to leap in the air. The whole thing was over in a couple of minutes – a nicely coordinated attack. When all the water had subsided, we found that no one was hurt. Luckily, the bombs had slightly delayed action fuses and had gone off rather deep. But several compartments were flooded including the Asdic compartment. This meant a dockyard job, for which Dover was in no way suitable.

So next day we were off to Chatham and out of the hot spot. Which was just as well because the next attack sank the *Codrington* (our new leader, with George Creasy in command – he survived) and the port had to be abandoned by destroyers. Repairs in Chatham took about ten days, so each watch had five days leave. There wasn't time to travel up to my parents, so I went down to Aldermaston to my Uncle Gerry Strange's, where I found all sorts of preparations being made for the expected invasion. Uncle Gerry, who had got a couple of DSOs in the First World War, was in khaki again as a Local Defence Volunteer – later and more appropriately called the Home Guard. He and some ex-Indian Army brigadiers were having a whale of a time fixing up tank traps in country lanes and amassing lead balls of a suitable size to be fired from double-barrelled shotguns. One night they went out on a patrol and were investigating a winking light in a farmhouse. Out came a barking dog, which was shot dead by an ex-Black-and-Tan major.

The farmer turned out to be quite innocuous. I've since felt that the squad must have been disappointed that the Germans never came. I have a happy memory of lying on the lawn at Bramley where I stayed a night with the Illingworths in the utmost luxury surrounded by dogs and cushions, looking at the poplar trees swaying in the wind, and living for the moment. I also went up to London from Chatham, when possible. At that time the trains were running normally. I think we all had the feeling that one must live the life while one could, and I believe that it was on this break that Jon Walley got married.

For me, I had a lot of fun and drank and smoked a lot. I remember taking Faith, who was unwise enough to marry me five years later, to the movies, where my hand shook so much that she had to help me light my cigarette. My last night in London culminated in a rather shameful episode when, having done the round of a lot of pubs, sampling sherry with my old friend Antony Lawrie, I found myself incapable of further progress. Antony had left and I was sitting in the dark in uniform on the steps of our last port of call, wondering how on earth (which was gyrating a bit) I'd ever get back to Chatham. Then a man appeared and asked me where I wanted to go. He got a taxi, came in it with me to Victoria Station, installed me in a room, arranged for me to be called in time for the first morning train, and made sure I had a ticket. He then vanished, refusing to give me his name or address and having paid the bill. I'm sure he was the Good Samaritan reincarnated. I duly caught the train, feeling poorly, to find the ship was under sailing orders. I doubt if I deserved my luck and it was a Friday too, 2 August 1940.

Mohamed Ali El Kebir

This time it was back to Plymouth, but not for long. One night in and we were off up the Irish Sea, bound for the Mediterranean. This was quite a surprise, and it must be admitted, a relief that we were to be away from the English Channel. On the other hand, we had been so much geared up to meet the invasion that it would be sad to miss it; at least we would have had something to shoot at instead of just being a target all the time. But – what will be will be. And at least the water would be warm.

Off the Clyde we picked up a troopship, the *Mohamed Ali El Kebir* (the Great), stuffed full of troops. We were the only escort that could be spared, so we took station ahead, zigzagging as usual across the line of advance and 'pinging' away. All went well until just before dark when there was an explosion – not a big one – right aft in the *Mohamed* and she started to sink slowly by the stern. Although not absolutely certain, we felt she had probably been hit by a torpedo.[7] The water was rather deep for a mine, and sabotage seemed unlikely. So, after circling the wreck searching for a U-boat, we closed her as she sank and started to pickup survivors, of whom there were many.

I'm sure most destroyer people have experienced that very naked feeling when you are stopped in the dark, a sitting target for a U-boat, which by now will have reloaded his torpedoes. And quite a number of ships have been lost in this way. I well remember feeling acutely uncomfortable; the asdic regularly giving its reverberating ping and no firm echoes returning, all on the bridge glued to binoculars, and Tony Juniper on the iron deck trying to embark hundreds of wet soldiers without showing a light. Luckily, most of them had got away in the boats, so we moved from boat to boat, occasionally doing a circuit to scare off our U-boat. At this, of course, the remaining boats thought they were being abandoned and yelled and flashed lights, which didn't help the feeling of nakedness. Inevitably, we were pulling one lot aboard when a lookout reported a periscope on the beam. So quickly full ahead leaving a lot of unhappy survivors behind. It was probably a false alarm, and we returned later.

It was a miserable night but by dawn we had got nearly all of them – 873 in all; I think, a record for our ship. They turned out to be reinforcements for the garrison of Gibraltar, and included a group of Canadian hard rock miners who were to bore tunnels in the Rock. They were urgently needed and only had a day's turn round in the Clyde before going out again.[8]

By now, the weather had turned thick, with visibility of no more than a mile. As navigator I was concerned about our position as we had wandered about quite a lot and the currents were uncertain. As we set course for the Clyde going easterly, we sounded regularly, but had to go faster than was navigationally prudent. When at last some grey land loomed up ahead there was doubt whether it was Scotland or Ireland. If Scotland, we should turn quickly to starboard; if Ireland, even more quickly to port. Breakers were visible, and above them a white building. At this moment Jon Walley, the doctor, a yachtsman of experience, arrived on the bridge. 'Ah, Islay!' he intoned. 'Of course, Doc,' we said deviously. He was right, and we turned right and all was well.

Gibraltar

A quick turnaround in the Clyde and we were off again on the 11th, this time with a southbound convoy. Apart from some thick fog and some encounters with ships that turned out to be friendly the trip was without incident. We secured alongside in the destroyer 'pens' in Gibraltar on the 18th. And what a relief it was to be in that relaxing climate with skies clear – at least for the moment – of our old friends the Me.s, Ju.s and He.s. But for all the relaxed tension, the days did not allow much rest. Next day we were out on the Straits patrol with the main object of preventing U-boats from entering the Mediterranean. In this, we were joined by our remaining flotilla-mates, *Greyhound*, *Gallant* and a number of destroyers from Force H under Admiral Sir James Somerville.

The situation in Gibraltar, though peaceful, was becoming tense. It was expected that the Germans would attack through Spain, especially if the invasion of England were postponed. The Spaniards were distinctly unfriendly and the French by now even more so. We were very much on our own. We did not know that Hitler's meeting with General Franco was to prove abortive. In any case, the French were an immediate problem. Since the attack on their fleet at Mers el Kebir in July, they had virtually become enemies, sending aircraft over Gibraltar frequently, occasionally to drop bombs. But they didn't bother us on our Straits patrols, which were on the whole delightful; warm, sunny and peaceful. A nice way to spend a war.

There were also some interesting incidents to keep up our morale. Opportunity was taken to practice gunnery and torpedo shoots at which we had become pretty rusty, having by now had no practices for a year. Unlike Nelson's navy, our constant sea time tended to reduce technical efficiency, though it made good seamen of us. The general pattern was of three or four-day patrols followed by a day, or perhaps a night, in harbour, interspersed with operations with Force H either in the Atlantic or the Mediterranean. After the last few months, this routine seemed almost restful.

At the end of August, after a day or two out with the aircraft carriers (we now had the *Ark Royal* and the *Illustrious*, which had completed working up) we set off on Operation HATS (Hands Across the Sea). This was an intricate operation mainly designed to pass reinforcements to Malta and the Eastern Mediterranean. In the three-day passage to Malta there were several air attacks by the Italians who tended to fly high in large formations, letting go a great forest of bomb splashes, rarely hitting anything. Out on the screen we felt pretty safe as they were after the big ships. In addition, our fighters were able to shoot down most of the shadowing aircraft and to put the bombing formations off their stroke. One almost felt sorry for the Italians who were mainly very brave men. Their shadowing aircraft in particular were firetraps, and easy meat, even for our indifferent fighters. However, one had to be constantly alert and it didn't do to be separated from the main body.

After passing the *Illustrious* and *Valiant* through to the east, the main part of Force H turned back while we went on to Malta and fuelled in Marsaxlokk harbour. Our night was rudely interrupted by a summons to chase an Italian motor torpedo boat, which had long gone by the time we reached the area. Then, a few hours in Boat House Creek and back to Gibraltar in the evening. It was well to go as fast as possible through the Cape Bon narrows so as to be as far west as possible by dawn. All went well until the following afternoon when the bombing attacks started, with we four destroyers the only target. This was no great problem as they still bombed from high up and one could see the clusters of white silvery bombs on the way down and had a good chance of avoiding them. On the bridge, we had a phlegmatic skipper of a Finnish ship who, for some reason, was taking passage. He was quite unmoved, taciturn, and ate a lot. Late in the afternoon the *Garland* (now repaired after her mishap in the early days, and manned by Poles) broke down and we had to turn back to tow her. We were now of course sitting ducks, still within range of the air base at Cagliari. None of us had radar, and we searched the skies a little anxiously until dark. But no further attacks developed. *Garland* got going again and we returned happily to Gibraltar.

French Fiasco

On one of the next Straits patrols occurred an incident which went into the history books. We were out with one of our chummy ships, the *Hotspur* who was senior to us. A little before 0500 we sighted three French cruisers, which turned out to be the *Gloire*, *Montcalm* and *Georges Leygues* (George's legs, to us). They were approaching the Straits from the east at high speed. *Hotspur* reported them and we started to shadow. No one knew what were their intentions, but it was clear that something was up. After an hour or two shadowing we were ordered back to Gibraltar. Normally we were not allowed to provoke incidents with French warships but had to stop and examine their merchant ships. However, we found it hard to understand why we were not allowed to continue to shadow. We were only in harbour long enough to refuel and were off again in pursuit, this time with *Renown*, flying Admiral Somerville's flag. By now the Frenchmen were well away and although we cast down towards Casablanca, we never caught up with them. In fact, they went on to Dakar, at that time the objective of the abortive British Free French expedition, carrying no less a person than Charles de Gaulle. The result was a fiasco and among other repercussions, the Flag Officer, Gibraltar, Admiral North, was relieved and sent home. Books have been written about this matter, which did not reflect well on the Admiralty or even Churchill himself. Many years later, after representations by several Admirals of the Fleet, Admiral North obtained a sort of exoneration, but a bad taste has remained.

A few days later, we were bombed again – this time by our late allies the French, who were still in a vindictive mood. One had the feeling, though, that the hearts of some of their airmen were not wholly in it. I must admit to some small feeling of satisfaction in being out at sea and watching the base being attacked. I felt that somehow it might sharpen them up a bit – an unworthy thought, no doubt.

Some Italian Submarines

Patrols continued as before. Every ship had to be investigated and as many were Spanish, some French and some neutral, discretion was required. On one occasion, we went out into the Atlantic to pick up survivors of a Yugoslav ship, the *Orao*, which had been torpedoed and was sinking very slowly with a cargo of wood. To our surprise, she had on board an officer and twelve men from the *Hotspur* who had boarded her earlier. They were glad to see us.

On another occasion, we went out to hunt an Italian submarine whose patrol line we knew. This was because her sister ship, the *Durbo*, had just been sunk and a boarding party had snatched her charts and operation orders just before she went under. After several hours 'pinging' with three destroyers, we found her and started depth charging. Maddeningly, nothing much happened for a long time. Then at last she broke surface and we lay bows to, waiting for the crew to bail out. Nothing of the sort. A moment or two later she disappeared again and we had a job to locate her. Then up she came again and this time *Hotspur* went for her and rammed. This was not a popular proceeding because it meant putting a destroyer out of action for a while (but the crew liked it). As the submarine sank, out came a ragged lot of survivors, to be picked up by *Gallant*. She reported that the submarine was called *Lafolè* (the one we were after) and that she had tried to surrender the first time she surfaced, but the conning tower hatch jammed shut! The captain was rescued. He was suffering from gonorrhoea. He was probably glad to be treated somewhere less embarrassing than his own base.

Our last encounter with Italian U-boats was rather strange. On 4 November we were off Tangier when we sighted a U-boat on the surface. Off we went after her, but found that she was already within Spanish territorial waters, so we could do nothing but read her name (*Bianchi*) and gnash our teeth as she slipped into Tangier. While waiting for her to come out again the following day, the same thing happened again. This time it was the *Brin*. A party from *Hotspur*, being repaired after the ramming, managed to get ashore in Tangier on leave, walk along the jetty and get a good look at our foes – an unusual experience in modern war. It turned out that we couldn't wait for them to emerge because all available destroyers were needed for the next fleet operation a day or two later. I believe they both escaped.

Gibraltar Again

Early in October we went into dock for routine boiler cleaning and repairs, a blissful time spent lying in the sun, swimming, playing tennis, sleeping, drinking, and, of course, doing paper work. There were virtually no girls on the Rock at this time. But at one stage the lovely and vivacious daughter of the recent British consul at Tunis came through. The French had evicted him, and his family were off to England in the next convoy. Someone in our wardroom was sharp enough to get her down for a drink or two. She coped admirably with the horde of officers from neighbouring ships; moths to a flame, poor chaps. At last, she said that she must be off to dine at Government House.

> 'But there's lots of time.'
> 'No, I must bath first.'
> 'We have a bath on board, with lots of hot water.'
> 'Well, why not?'

It turned out that we hadn't, so she went next door to the *Gallant*'s bath. Now, the captain of the *Gallant*, a most efficient officer who had been flag lieutenant to a commander-in-chief, had started to go a little off balance with the strain of war. He required a state of perfection, unattainable in wartime, and didn't care for women smoking or drinking, other than sherry. He now happened to return on board to find a naked woman in his bath, with a posse of drinking, smoking officers handing her sponges and towels through the door. The first lieutenant was placed under open arrest for allowing it to happen and the officer of the day likewise for being on duty at the time. It took all the blandishments of Johnny L-B and Neville Currey, the captain of the *Wrestler*, also alongside, to have the matter overlooked. Neville Currey, who was relieved shortly afterwards in the ordinary course of events, took passage to England in the same ship as our lovely lady, married her and lived happily ever after.

Things like this have always tended to happen in Gibraltar, and destroyer life in those days still tended to breed a certain kind of autocrat. One such was Roland Swinley, about whom many stories are told. He was captain of the *Douglas* at this time. He had been down to our wardroom and stayed very late, drinking sherry. As we hadn't invited him to dinner, he said in a rather menacing way:

> 'I can see you don't like me.'
> 'Of course we love you, sir.'
> 'Then you shall dine with me.'
> 'But it is far too late,' (it must have been around midnight).
> 'Dinner is when I say it is.'

So we trooped over to the *Douglas* which, indeed, had been through this kind of thing before. And sure enough there was a meal ready. Roland sat in silence throughout until a rather burnt savoury was placed in front of him. Without hesitation, he reached for the quartermaster's bell.

> 'Sir?'
> 'Quartermaster, who is officer of the day?'

Brasher was roused from sleep, and appeared in a dressing gown. This might have been a mistake, but was a good guess this time.

'Are you officer of the day?'

'Yes, sir.'

'Eat my savoury.'

He made a pretty speech of acceptance, which made it all seem quite a natural occurrence. Poor Brasher was lost not long after.

Before leaving Gibraltar, mention should be made of Admiral Sir James Somerville who led Force H. He was a great man with a tremendous power of instilling confidence, and an irrepressible sense of humour. He used to row around the harbour early in the morning in a little dinghy by himself, and was quite likely to appear suddenly on one's quarterdeck to have a look around. He seemed to be given many of the dirty jobs, such as Oran and later the Eastern Fleet, and was not well treated by the Admiralty or Churchill. Too independent, perhaps. He should have been given a title, in our opinion. His son John was in my term and became a successful civil servant at GCHQ after the war. He and I used to listen to music together during the air raids on Alexandria.

Moving East

Our time at Gibraltar came to an end on 7 November, when we left with Force H on another operation, which would see *Greyhound*, *Gallant* and ourselves, along with the battleship *Barham* and two cruisers pass into the eastern Mediterranean. Before we left, it became time for Tony Juniper, the first lieutenant, to be relieved, as he was due for a command of his own. Johnny was kind enough to offer me his place and I accepted with some pride but with no small feeling of inadequacy due to my inexperience. To be second-in-command of a fleet destroyer was pretty good going in those days for someone only 22 years old. When we got out to Alexandria I found myself vastly junior to all my opposite numbers, but as we were at sea so much it didn't become very apparent, especially as Johnny and the wardroom generally were superb – in particular, Florrie Foord who had more experience than most of us put together. Jack Fenn-Clark who was now the 'chief' had been my engineering instructor in the training cruiser in 1935, but never for a moment showed any resentment at one so young being mess president. To make up our numbers we received Henry Trefusis, a most delightful and entertaining RNVR lieutenant, whose squeezebox and stock of songs of all kinds kept us amused until much too late at night.

With these changes duly effected, we set off with the fleet, escorting a convoy to Malta. It was the usual story for those days: shadowing Italians, mostly shot down by *Ark Royal's* fighters; eventually the inevitable high-level bombing attacks, impressive but singularly unlucky in that their huge forests of bomb explosions rarely hit anything. To hit a moving ship you must come low and this the Italians wouldn't do except for their torpedo bombers who were wonderfully brave, but too slow and vulnerable to be much of a menace. They had a horrid way of bursting into flames when hit, then plunging into the blue Mediterranean in a puff of black smoke and oil.

On the 10th, we passed Cape Bon and that morning came in sight of the Eastern Mediterranean fleet, our spiritual home and a splendid and inspiring sight under Admiral A.B. Cunningham. It was good to be with him again. A quick nip into the Grand Harbour for fuel, then back to rejoin and make off eastward. Next night, 11 November, became famous in Fleet Air Arm history – the attack on Taranto. We on the screen could only watch the old *Swordfish* trundling heavily off the *Illustrious*, and later count them when they returned in the dark.

It seemed pretty good and indeed it was. None the less, one couldn't help feeling that our proportions were wrong: one aircraft carrier to five battleships. If it had been the other way round we could have held the Mediterranean in the months to come, to say nothing of Norway and Singapore. The loss of the Royal Naval Air Service in 1918 was, to my thinking, a disaster of the first magnitude. The next few days saw some more bombing attacks but we never felt much worried about them, as even our slow 'Fulmar' fighters could cope well enough.

Alexandria

On 14 November 1940 we arrived in Alexandria after an absence of eleven months. There at our buoy to welcome us was Achmed Squiffi, our feluccaman. The Gyppy grapevine had warned him and he came on board with the candle lantern which we had had to leave on board as a battle practice target when we had left for the UK in 1939. We almost hugged him, toothless grin and all.

ABC never let us stay long in harbour, and we were off a couple of days later on a series of intricate operations, largely concerned with setting up a base in Suda Bay, Crete, passing convoys to Malta, Greece and Palestine, and making air attacks on Italian air bases on the route to Greece, who was now an ally since the Italian attack on her in October. On one of the Malta runs we broke down in mid-ocean and were left on our own for a couple of hours – and a very naked feeling it was to be stopped with no-one else in sight, and the usual threat of aircraft or U-boats. However, the engine room staff got us going again, and as a result we were sent into Malta for docking and repairs.

Air attacks on the island were already quite heavy but nothing like what they later became. One day some of us went up to the RAF base at Luqa for lunch. We put down our gins when a large formation of bombers flew over. As the bombs descended, we all popped into a shelter, and when they had exploded, went on with our gins. All in all things felt pretty good, and we had some memorable evenings in the bowling alleys, drinking beer and eating scrambled eggs. December was a halcyon month for the Mediterranean Fleet. The Italian surface fleet – still much stronger on paper – wasn't prepared to meet the fire-eating ABC again. Their U-boats hadn't proved to be too much of a problem, and with our noble *Illustrious* there wasn't too much to fear from the air. In short, we were masters of the sea, coming and going as we pleased. There were some superb days at sea – brilliant sun, cool air, clear visibility and dark blue seas. Sometimes even today, similar conditions take my mind back there. Of course, it could be rough and unpleasant, but the change from the winter North Sea was delightful.

We spent very little time in harbour – rarely more than a day or two at a time, soon falling into the routine of the Mediterranean fleet, which was perhaps at its peak efficiency at this period. ABC was always at sea in the *Warspite* and one felt that his sharp blue eye was on every manoeuvre. In fact, I only set eyes on him once, when he came on board without warning in Alexandria harbour. He only spent a few minutes with us, talked to Jamie the bull terrier, who was always polite to senior officers, and went off in his barge like a breath of sharp and invigorating air. He did have to revise one opinion though. When we first rejoined the fleet, Johnny made his call on the admiral. The subject of air attack was broached and ABC described the Italian high-level air attacks on the fleet so far. Johnny said that in his opinion the German Stukas were far more of a menace; we had seen both kinds in action. ABC wouldn't buy this, but time was to prove him wrong.

December was a busy month; back and forth to Malta and Greece and calling in at Suda Bay for fuel. Weather was sometimes rough. On one occasion we were lucky not to lose A.B. Bradley who was washed overboard, but recovered. On Christmas day, we were escorting a small convoy south of Melos, and felt secure enough to close the merchant vessels to sing them carols over the loud hailer.

Bardia

Returning to Alexandria on the 31st, we were off again on 2 January, this time to screen the *Warspite, Valiant, Barham* and *Illustrious* for the bombardment of Bardia, then surrounded by the Army of the Nile (later called the 8th Army). Hitherto naval support along the Libyan coast had been provided by some old China river gunboats and the ancient monitor *Terror*, which carried two 15" guns. These had fired so many shells that the rifling of their barrels had worn down with the result that her shells, instead of spinning in the usual way, went bounding over the desert like ducks and drakes – a much more effective terroriser than the normal shell.

Our performance was to pound the 25,000-strong Italian garrison to prevent them counter-attacking the Australians who were trying to take the port. We destroyers had to stream our 'Two Speed Destroyer Sweeps' (TSDS) a mass of wire knitting designed to cut a clear path through any moored minefield. It was my job as first lieutenant. Never having done it before, I was mighty glad of Florrie Foord's guiding hand, bless him. The assault took place on the 3rd and provided a fine sight, although one could see little result other than a huge cloud of yellow sand. A brave little shore battery replied with a few small shells, wide of the mark. Bardia fell that day, and we were back in Alexandria next evening.

Part III

Crisis in the Mediterranean

Change of Fortune

A couple of days later we were off again on Operation Excess, whose main object was to pass some more merchant ships through to Malta, Greece and back to Egypt. After fuelling in Suda we accompanied the fleet to a position west of Malta, in sight of Pantellaria, then reported to be bristling with batteries. It was on this day (the 10th) that the fortunes of the fleet changed and things started to get very rough.

We were busy changing the direction of the screen when our next-door neighbour, the *Gallant*, going at some thirty knots, hit a mine. Within a moment her bows disappeared and she lay stopped in the water. We hastened alongside to provide assistance, the weather being quite calm. The first thing that met us was a shower of Maltese suitcases, the wardroom cooks and stewards usually being ready packed for such an occasion. I don't mean to disparage their courage. Life was tough for them with their families besieged in Malta, now only just over the horizon but usually far away. One officer, who shall be nameless, calmly stuffed a pile of binoculars into a canvas bag and proceeded to jump aboard us with the bag in hand. It is possible that he hated to see naval stores lost, but unlikely. Anyhow, just as he was stepping from one iron deck to the other, the ships lurched apart and he dropped the binoculars into 500 fathoms. But at least he didn't get his feet wet.

Gallant did not need much help, actually. There was no fire and a destroyer will usually float quite nicely without a bow. But she had to be towed and we started to get ready. *Mohawk* was ordered to do this so we escorted them slowly towards Malta, covered by the cruisers *Gloucester*, *Southampton* and *Bonaventure* – all to be sunk ere long. It was a little uncomfortable steaming so close to the enemy's air base.

About lunchtime, the first wave of bombers went for the *Illustrious*. They were Ju.87s, our old friends from Norway. The German air force had appeared in the Mediterranean and life became unpleasant. The story of the *Illustrious* is well known. She survived, miraculously, and limped into Malta. Apart from desultory attacks we were left alone for the bigger game. But on arrival in Malta they berthed us immediately astern of the *Illustrious*. I must say I was anxious that we shouldn't be there for long as it was perfectly clear that the Germans wouldn't rest until they had sunk the carrier. We were altogether too close for comfort. The poor old *Gallant* came in safely but never went to sea again. That left *Greyhound* and ourselves out of our original nine.

Fortunately, we didn't stay long in that berth. Even as we left, the attacks started. But we had to raise steam for full speed to go to the rescue of the *Southampton* who had been bombed and set on fire east of Malta. She had been in company with *Gloucester* but neither of these fine ships had radar, so that an attack out of the sun by the expert Ju.87s caught them by surprise. *Gloucester* had been hit on the bridge and *Southampton* set on fire. It seemed only a short while ago that they had been covering us as we crept in with *Gallant*. Astern of *Mohawk* we set off at full speed. There was a declared 'dangerous area' due to mines right in our path. *Mohawk* went around it but Johnny decided that as we were slower, we'd take the risk of a short cut although *Mohawk* (Jack Eaton, senior to us) wouldn't give permission. The blind eye was successful. We came safely through and caught up. Sadly though, the *Southampton*'s blaze was uncontrollable. She had to be sunk before we reached the scene. So we went on to Suda Bay and refuelled.

The next few days were spent in the Aegean where the German air force had not yet penetrated. We screened the old

Eagle which, besides being an antique herself, had some very decrepit aircraft onboard and just could not be risked any nearer to Malta. Somehow whenever we came into harbour for a night's rest we seemed to be sailing again very early the next morning, off on another operation.

Gnat

When a last we got back to Alexandria on the 18th, we had no sooner fuelled from the oiler than we were out again into a full gale to stand by the *Gnat*, which was in trouble. She was one of the old China river gunboats, built for the Danube in the First World War and used ever since in the Yangtze River. She was shaped like a flatiron, only drawing a foot or two. Certainly she was not meant for heavy seas. We found her off the Nile Delta, drifting towards shore and unable to make headway against the wind and sea. We managed to smooth out the breaking crests by pouring oil from bags trailing over the side. I must say I felt very sick what with the heavy seas and my lungs full of little droplets of oil fuel – a foul smell at the best of times and which to this day I associate with survivors swimming in the water. The weather being so thick and the land around the Rosetta mouths of the Nile being so flat and featureless, we were obliged to sound, using the old wire machine with a lead weight. Eventually after a very unpleasant day and night we managed to see the *Gnat* safely back to Alexandria and had a couple of nights in. My paintwork (not looking its best after all that sea time) was now covered in a coating of oil from masthead to waterline. It took a long time and a lot of work before we began to look respectable again.

Still the youngest first lieutenant in the flotilla (now the 14th), I had to try not to look scruffier than the others. Our leader, the *Jervis*, always managed a look of almost peacetime cleanliness, and I was envious. Her first lieutenant, Walter Scott, was rather a fanatic and most efficient in a humourless way. Our new Captain (D), Philip Mack, was quite superb, and one of the finest leaders I have ever met. Whenever he came onboard, our spirits lifted. He was a wonderful, experienced destroyer man and somehow achieved high standards of efficiency without appearing critical. We always felt that at sea he, if anyone, would pull us through. Later he was promoted to rear admiral and was lost in an aircraft accident. We lost a First Sea Lord.

Jervis survived the war, as did we. It is a pity that no such destroyers were later preserved for posterity.[9]

Red Sea Interlude

The rest of January was spent exercising. As by now we were rather rusty at anti-submarine work we were heartened to go out and meet the *Illustrious*, which had survived her ordeal and was cheered into Alexandria. Then, greatly to our surprise and delight we and *Juno* were ordered into the Red Sea to go and meet the *Formidable*, newly commissioned and now ready to take the place of *Illustrious*. So on 1 February 1941, we arrived at Port Said, through the Suez Canal and were in Aden on the 5th just as *Formidable* arrived from around the Cape. The next two weeks were spent with her in the Red Sea, working up. Although unpleasantly hot, it was relatively safe, as the Italians in Massawa seemed to have relapsed into inaction. In later years when I was sweeping the Red Sea minefields, I could see why. Massawa is the hot end of the earth, and utterly debilitating. We spent a day in Port Sudan, which was just as hot as it had been in 1939 when we were there at the outbreak of war. This time we had to be employed as an oil tanker because none were available and *Formidable* was too large to get near the fuelling jetty. Then there was a delay in getting us through the Suez Canal. The Germans had been using long-range aircraft to lay mines in the canal, and there had been much difficulty locating and sweeping them. Also, several ships had been sunk so that at one point it was only just possible to squeeze the great *Formidable* past. Once again, one kept one's knees a little bent past the dangerous areas; but all went well and we were back in Alexandria on the 10th.

Malta

After a brief docking in the Gabbari dock we were off again escorting a convoy. This time the fleet covered us for the first part of the journey, leaving the destroyers of the escort to go on through to Malta with the four merchant ships. These were the first relief for the garrison since our ill-fated efforts in early January. So they were much needed. As it turned out, we were not located, for which we had some foul weather to thank. We entered Grand Harbour on the morning of the 2nd, to find the battlements black with Maltese, in spite of an air raid warning. They gave us a tremendous reception, even going so far as to sing 'God Save the King', an anthem I had never before heard sung spontaneously.

We went straight up harbour to the Marsa, where we went alongside the oiling jetty at Ras Hanzir. The air attacks started very soon as evidently the enemy had woken up to the arrival of the convoy. We weren't menaced directly until the afternoon, when three Ju.87s came low down over the ridge above and aimed straight at us. There wasn't much we could do. Our two .5" machine guns were in action (for what they were worth, which wasn't much). I was on the bridge and grabbed an old Lewis gun, which we had acquired somewhere. The largest bomb came down right past the bridge, so close that I felt I could read the maker's name. It landed in the water about ten yards off, exploded on contact and filled us with dirty water and splinter holes – some 400 of them. Two of the .5" machine gunners, Carson and Walker, were badly hit. Walker died later – our first casualty since March 1940. They had gone on firing until hit themselves and richly deserved a medal. I was not so brave, and split my trousers up the seat in flinging myself onto the deck, more or less at the last moment. Sadly, even if the .5"s had got any hits, they would have had little effect, as we were to see later. We heard afterwards that examination of bits of the bomb showed that it was of British manufacture. But all the holes were superficial, only needing plugging with wooden pegs of various sizes. The ship was quite fit for sea and left that evening in company with an old friend, the *Bonaventure*, an anti-aircraft cruiser who by now had had plenty of practice. We reached Alexandria on the 24th without incident. Sad to relate, two of the four ships of our convoy were sunk in Malta that day.

It was round about now that we were joined by Mike Hennell, an RN lieutenant who had come round the Cape in a convoy which had been in an action with German surface ships on Christmas Day. Mike, of whom more anon, was a great asset to the ship. He had great charm, a lively sense of humour and an ability to draw appropriate cartoons.

Matapan

Three days later, it became clear that something else was in the wind. Shortly after dark, the whole fleet left harbour. The C-in-C was there in *Warspite* with *Valiant*, *Barham*, *Formidable* and nine destroyers, including ourselves. The subsequent action – the battle of Matapan – is well enough known. As far as we were concerned, the next day was full of signals reporting action by our cruisers against the Italian fleet. *Formidable* flew fighter and reconnaissance patrols, which kept us free of attacks except for one brave but unsuccessful effort by two Savoia torpedo bombers. At dusk, it appeared that there might be some chance of catching up with the Italian battleship *Vittoria Veneto*, which had been hit by a torpedo from *Formidable*'s aircraft. So *Jervis* and four of the screen were detached to speed ahead to look for her. Lucky devils, we thought.

We remained with our own battle feet as screen: *Stuart* (Captain (D)), *Greyhound*, *Griffin* and *Havock*. Our leader, *Stuart*, was an Australian destroyer commanded by that great character Hec Waller (later lost in the *Perth* in the Java Sea, fighting the Japanese). *Greyhound* and ourselves were to port, the other two to starboard. We were all at action stations. I was closed up in the director tower, being gunnery control officer, and in a good position to see everything.

We were steaming into a black night at twenty knots, peering into the darkness through our binoculars. Suddenly we received an emergency signal to clear the screen and take station on the starboard side. Increasing to full speed, we started off, to receive in short order another signal from *Warspite*: GET OUT OF MY WAY, DAMN YOU. At this moment, I spotted a dark shape ahead and got all the guns onto it. As we got nearer, it was obviously a large ship and one felt a little naked up there in front. Moments later, *Greyhound*, ahead of us, switched on her searchlight and in its silvery-blue beam was revealed a 10,000-ton cruiser heading towards us, quite close, and looking magnificent in her light grey, which stood out starkly in the beam. I gave an estimated range and opened fire. 'Ting-ting' went the firing bell. Then hell broke loose. The enemy ship virtually disintegrated in an appalling series of explosions, flinging one of her turrets high in the air. 'My God, did I do that?' was my first reaction, forgetting that there were three battleships behind us.[10]

A few seconds later a couple of Italian destroyers appeared, and as they were clearly our job, we went off after them. I got a few salvoes off but they had the legs of us and soon vanished, though another pair was sunk by *Stuart* and *Havock*. After pursuing our two, *Greyhound* and ourselves took a cast ahead, hoping to happen upon the damaged battleship. We found nothing, though had we been fitted with radar it is quite likely that we would have picked her up, as she was not very far away. As it was we hustled off into the darkness. C-in-C recalled us. Having himself turned away after his action we reduced speed somewhat and sadly started back. After about an hour, when one was beginning to tire, the bridge sighted a darkened ship ahead. At once, we were alert, finger on the trigger. If it was the battleship, we could expect a massive salvo as soon as she spotted us. But equally we had a good chance to slip a fish into her. Our torpedoes were already trained on the beam. *Greyhound* and ourselves reduced speed, keeping bows onto the enemy to reduce our visibility from her. As we drew nearer, it became clear that something very odd was going on. A destroyer was close to a large ship on which flashing lights could be seen, moving about the decks. Once again, *Greyhound* shone her searchlight. Once again it revealed a light grey, 10,000-ton cruiser, lying stopped with her guns trained fore and aft. Then we could see that amidships she was glowing red and the decks were crammed with men. Obviously she was in no condition to fight, and the destroyer with her was one of our own – the *Havock*. We were just getting ready to go alongside and do an old-fashioned boarding party when Captain Mack in *Jervis* appeared on the scene. When we announced our intention of boarding we got a short reply: 'No, I will.' So we didn't have that pleasure and had to content ourselves with picking up a large number of Italian sailors who were floating in the water astern.

Their morale was shot to ribbons. Many were drunk. It turned out that this was the *Pola*, one of the three cruisers we had encountered. She had been hit by a torpedo from the *Formidable*'s aircraft earlier in the day, and stopped. The other two cruisers had been sent to her assistance and had just established contact when our battle fleet blew them to pieces. The *Pola* was already on fire down below and her crew were quite shattered by this experience. They had lost power, couldn't fire their guns and were expecting a similar fate at any minute. One sailor whom we picked up had on three lifebelts, all round his hindquarters, so he had been having trouble keeping his mouth above water. He spoke some English. When asked about his experiences he said that he heard a huge explosion, said to himself 'Mama Mia! I cannot swim!', and dived overboard. Our ship's company formed a poor opinion of the survivors who complained about our food. Next morning the coxswain represented to me that our sailors wanted to throw them back. This request had to be refused.

Bonaventure

After the night's excitements we rejoined the fleet, underwent some desultory bombing, and were detached to Piraeus to land our prisoners.

With some pride we went alongside the *Grimsby* displaying our trophies and the 400 holes in our hull and upperworks. The battle, satisfactory though it had been, was disappointing in that we didn't get the *Vittoria Veneto*. Nor did we, in *Griffin*, get a chance to fire our torpedoes. But we couldn't complain, having had a bloodless victory (except for the crew of a Swordfish).

After fuelling in Piraeus we were off straight away escorting a convoy to Alexandria. By now, the British were starting to ship men and materials in quantity to Greece unfortunately to the detriment of our own cause in the Western Desert, a lack of which we were to feel in the next few months. On this occasion the ships were returning empty. Things seemed reasonably in hand; there was even some fighter protection, so our spirits remained high. But just before 0300 next morning there was a heavy explosion astern. The brave *Bonaventure* had been torpedoed and sank very rapidly with great loss of life. We started off to her assistance, or at least to pick up survivors, but were ordered back to the convoy. This incident was doubly sad. We lost an old comrade who had so often beaten off air attacks; and, although we didn't know it at the time, this represented the appearance of submarines on the scene (this one was Italian). Hitherto the Italians hadn't bothered us too much, and our main worries had been from the air.

Red Sea Again

However, one lived for the moment, and the next few days, to our surprise, took us down to the Red Sea again. The British armies were at last extinguishing the Italian Empire in East Africa. They were advancing on the Naval Base at Massawa where there lay a flotilla of destroyers and several submarines. No one knew what they would do when driven out of their last anchorage, so in company with *Greyhound* and *Kimberley* we were to meet them if they came north.

So, delivering our convoy to Alexandria, we went straight on to Port Said and once again through the Suez Canal, now reputed to be clear of mines. But it was 1 April and one couldn't be sure so we proceeded gingerly. At that time someone had the idea of stretching nets over the canal in the awkward places so that a falling mine would make a hole in the net and reveal its position. Egyptian nets being what they were, there must have been many false alerts. We spent a few rather blissful days cruising down the Red Sea, spread apart at visibility distance, ready for what we expected would be an easy victory. But on the 5th we heard that all eight enemy destroyers had been sunk or put out of action by *Eagle*'s aircraft operating from Port Sudan. So we were robbed of cheap glory.

The next day we were back through the canal, our brief rest from eternal vigilance over.

Sollum

The news that day was not good. The Germans had invaded Yugoslavia and Greece. Rommel's forces had pushed eastwards beyond Tobruk and it was not certain how far they had progressed. We were granted three days in Alexandria, one of which was spent going over the degaussing range to make sure our demagnetization against mines was satisfactory. Then on the 11th we went off westwards with the cruisers to cover merchant shipping movements to Greece and to pass the *Jervis* and three other destroyers to Malta, where they were to operate against the enemy's convoys to Libya. The situation in the desert was becoming desperate, and London was putting great pressure on ABC to do something drastic, including even a scheme to sink the *Barham* as a blockship in Tripoli harbour. Fortunately ABC resisted such an impracticable scheme. The Malta flotilla under P.J. Mack did very well, but lost the fine *Mohawk*; Jack Eaton, later my captain after the war, had to swim for it.

On the way back from this outing, *Stuart* and ourselves were detached to Sollum to find out what the military situation was. It was confused. We approached the sandy coast at dawn, rather cautiously. Halfaya Pass was readily identified as we closed the beach, ready to anchor, or not, as circumstances dictated. We started to make signals to the army ashore, to be instantly rewarded by shellfire from various types of mobile guns. Evidently, the wrong side was in possession, so we retired to sea a little way and started to reply.

This was rather fun. As gunnery control officer, I could see tanks along the road. We opened the range so that they couldn't reply and started to shoot them up. It was nice to clobber the German army for a change instead of being a target for their air force. Unfortunately, a destroyer's high-muzzle velocity gun is not well adapted for such work and it was hard to hit anything with accuracy. After a while there was so much sand and dust that I couldn't see the targets. So ended our first taste of bombardment – not very effective, but fun. We managed to establish where the front line was without much difficulty after which we went beetling back to Alexandria, arriving at dawn next day, the 15th, for three lovely nights.

Tripoli

Meanwhile, unknown to us, a war of telegrams had been going on between ABC and Churchill who seemed to have little idea of how hard pressed we were, trying with a limited number of ships to keep Malta and Greece supplied, to support the army in the desert, all in the face of air attack against which there was little defence but a handful of fighters in the *Formidable* which could only be in one place at a time. When the carrier was not present you could be sure that any aircraft sighted was hostile. In addition, the U-boats were becoming a menace and the narrow waters were plentifully strewn with mines. Eventually ABC agreed, with misgivings, to take the fleet to bombard Tripoli harbour – a rash venture to say the least.

The operation was well planned. A convoy was run out of Malta; the *Breconshire,* a fast, supply ship, supported by cruisers, ran fuel into Malta while the fleet proceeded as if to cover these rather usual operations; the idea being to turn after dark to Tripoli, make a surprise bombardment and be well off the coast by dawn. Destroyers were to mine sweep ahead of the fleet when it reached mineable waters. *Formidable* was to eliminate shadowing aircraft and provide fighter cover for the retirement.

We sailed early in the morning of 18 April 1941. All went remarkably well. I don't think the enemy ever spotted the fleet. Most of their aircraft may well have been fully occupied in Greece and the Western Desert. On the evening before the bombardment we were detached, with mixed feelings, to screen *Formidable*; a less dangerous but also less interesting role than sweeping ahead of the battleships. So we missed the fireworks, which were spectacular, we heard, though I doubt if there was great interference with Rommel's supplies. Next morning, the 21st, we all joined up and the fleet returned to Alexandria. Sailing right into the enemy's home waters, we had expected trouble, but nothing happened.

Greece

About noon on the 22nd, instead of returning to Alexandria, *Kandahar* and we were detached to Suda Bay, Crete. The army was in trouble in Greece. Although we didn't know it, the decision to evacuate had already been taken. The whole affair had always sounded crazy to us. To denude our forces in the desert just when Rommel had arrived; to add a huge maritime burden to our already over-extended fleet; and to set an ill-equipped army ashore in a small country to face an overwhelming display of armoured might, in the face of complete air superiority – the end result could

Alec Dennis as a naval cadet. (*Dennis family album*)

Alec Dennis on leave. (*Dennis family album*)

Midshipman Dennis. (*Dennis family album*)

Midshipman Dennis. (*Dennis family album*)

British G Class destroyer HMS *Griffin*. Transferred to the Royal Canadian Navy as HMC Ottawa (H31) in 1943. (*Imperial War Museum. Crown copyright expired*)

HMS *Griffin*. (*Hugh Knollys*)

Men of the Polish Podhalan Rifles Brigade, 1940. *Polish official photographer, Imperial War Museum. Crown copyright expired*)

German Junkers Ju 87B Stuka dive bomber, c.1940. *US Navy Naval Aviation News, 1 September 1943. Public Domain*)

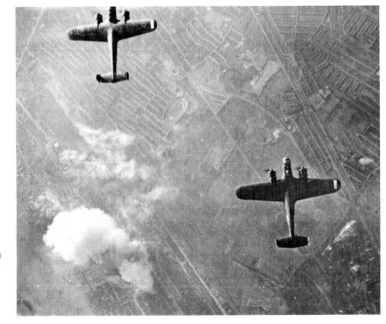

Two Dornier Do 17 bombers over West Ham, London, flying above fires started by bombs in the neighbourhood of Beckton gas works. (*Royal Air Force official photographer. Crown copyright expired*)

Admiral of the Fleet Sir Charles Forbes (front left) with Polish naval officers. (*Admiralty official collection, Lt L. Pelman, Imperial War Museum. Crown copyright expired*)

Three Lysander Mark Is, L4721, L4728 and L4715, of No. 208 Squadron RAF, based at Heliopolis, Egypt, entering a port turn after flying over the Suez Canal. (*Air Ministry Second World War official collection, Royal Air Force official photographer*)

The evacuation from Greece, 1941. Soldiers climbing over the side of a boat into a waiting rowing boat at night. In the water behind them is another boat with a single figure holding a torch. (*H. Johns, Imperial War Museum. Crown copyright expired*)

Burning ships in the harbour at Suda Bay, Crete, 25 June 1941. (*Australian photo unit, Imperial War Museum. Crown copyright expired*)

(*Left*) Admiral of the Fleet, Sir Andrew Browne Cunningham, Commander-in-Chief, Mediterranean Fleet, 1940-43. (*Royal Navy official photographer, Admiralty official collection, Imperial War Museum*)

(*Below*) Admiral Cunningham saluting as the morning colours are hoisted on board HMS *Queen Elizabeth*, docked in Alexandria Harbour. (*Royal Navy official photographer Lt E.A. Zimmerman, Imperial War Museum. Crown copyright expired*)

Heavy bomb damage in Kingsway, Valletta, Malta, 1 May 1942. Service personnel and civilians are clearing up the debris. (*Official Royal Navy photographer Lt J.E. Russell, Imperial War Museum. Crown copyright expired*)

The battleship HMS *Queen Elizabeth* in Alexandria Harbour surrounded by anti-torpedo nets, c.1939-45. (*Royal Navy official photographer, Imperial War Museum. Crown copyright expired*)

Aboard the SS *Queen Mary*, around a conference table sit Prime Minister Winston Churchill, Field Marshal Sir Archibald P. Wavell, GCB, CMG, MC, and Admiral Sir James Somerville, KCB, KBE, DSO. (*Royal Navy official photographer Lt H.W. Tomlin, Imperial War Museum. Crown copyright expired*)

The British Royal Navy battleship HMS *Barham* (04) explodes as her 15-inch magazine ignites. (*Film still. Official photograph*)

Members of the Japanese Imperial Navy Midget Submarine Attack Group who carried out simultaneous attacks on Diego Suarez (Madagascar) and Sydney Harbour in 1942. (*Author unknown, Australian War Memorial*)

General views of the warships and British merchant ships in harbour at Diego Suarez after the French (Vichy) had surrendered in 1942. (*RN official photographer Lt S.J. Beadell, Imperial War Museum. Crown copyright expired*)

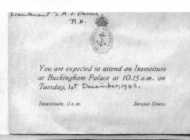

(*Left*) Alec pictured with his parents receiving his DSC. (*Dennis family album*)

(*Below*) U570, a Type VIIC submarine, in 1943. (*UK Government, Imperial War Museum. Crown copyright expired*)

Looking weather-battered and worn, the destroyer HMS *Savage* enters Scapa Flow after the Battle of the North Cape, which resulted in the sinking of the *Scharnhorst*. (*Royal Navy official photographer Lt H.A. Mason*)

A welcome moment of relaxation. (*Dennis family album*)

(*Above left*) Mr A.V. Alexander, First Lord of the Admiralty, on a visit to the Home Fleet, January 1943. Left to right: Rear Admiral Robert Burnett, the Right Honourable A.V. Alexander and Admiral Sir John Tovey on board the cruiser HMS *Belfast*. (Imperial War Museum. Crown copyright expired)

(*Above right*) Ernest Bevin, Minister of Labour. (*British Government. Crown copyright expired*)

(*Below*) The British comedian Tommy Handley rehearses with actors from his ITMA show and the Royal Marines band during a visit to the Home Fleet at Scapa Flow, January 1944. (*Royal Navy official photographer Lt H.A. Mason*)

The campaign in Normandy, June 1944. Tracer fire from HM ships streaking the darkness as an almost impenetrable screen is put up against the enemy bombers during a night bombing attack at the anchorage at Ouistreham off Normandy. Photograph taken on board HMS *Mauritius*, 10 June 1944. (*Royal Navy official photographer Lt W.E. Rolfe, Imperial War Museum. Crown copyright expired*)

British aircraft carriers HMS *Indomitable* (R92), HMS *Indefatigable* (R10), HMS *Unicorn* (I72), HMS *Illustrious* (R87), HMS *Victorious* (R38) and HMS *Formidable* (R67) at anchor, with other shipping. (*Royal Navy, Imperial War Museum. Crown copyright expired*)

Alec Dennis, Lord Teynham and Brigadier Mike Calvert arrive at Kristiansand, May 194
(*Dennis family album*)

HMS *Valorous*. (*Hugh Knollys*)

Hunt class destroyer HMS *Tetcott* on a convoy to Russia. (*Royal Navy Official photographer Imperial War Museum. Crown copyright expired*)

HMS *Tetcott*, Gibraltar, September 1945. (*Dennis family album*)

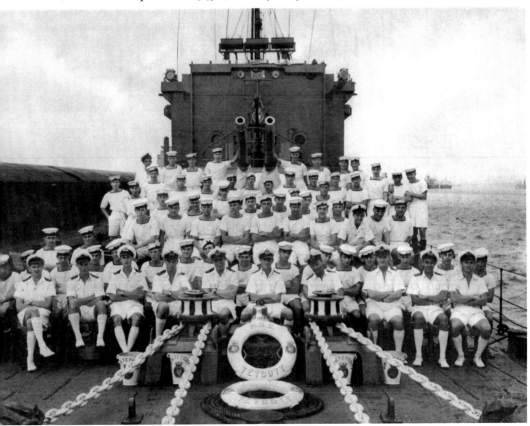

Alec Dennis, aged 90, taken at his home in West Vancouver. (*Dennis family album*)

have been (and was) predicted by any one of us. But the politicians insisted and we had to pay. There were, of course, arguments in favour of our intervention, not least of which was simple loyalty to our Greek allies who fought well until overwhelmed, and certainly greeted us with open arms.

So on the evening of 22 April we entered Suda Bay to fuel. A sad sight was the cruiser *York* sitting on the bottom, having been torpedoed while in harbour by a most daring Italian fast motorboat. The submarine *Rover* lay alongside her to provide power, but in the end the *York* stayed there to be bombed and abandoned when we lost Crete. Air raid warnings Yellow followed by Red seemed to be the order of the day, so our solitary 3" a-a gun was continuously manned by day.

A couple of hours to fuel and we were off at twenty-five knots to join the first evacuation convoy, on its way to Megara. We joined them next afternoon and were gratified to find them accompanied by the anti-aircraft cruiser *Coventry*, which could at least deter air attack. The convoy consisted of the liners *Pennland* and *Thurland Castle*, escorted by ourselves, *Diamond* and *Wryneck*. Attacks were only sporadic that afternoon but there were many alerts. By next afternoon they became more severe and more frequent, until at last at 1400 when we were off San Georgio island one of the convoy was hit – the fairly large Dutch liner *Pennland*. We were ordered to close her to assist.

At 1530 she was leaking quite badly but capable of steaming. We had hopes of getting her to Megara, but later she became unmanoeuvrable. We closed her and as we did so at about 1800 there was another air attack. She was hit again and we were narrowly missed by a bomb which fell between us. As was so often the case in those days, a brilliant sun shone out of a clear blue sky, so that it was very hard to spot these pests on their way down. This time, the only warning was the scream of the descending bombs.

Again, as always, I used to watch the sun, falling ever so gradually to the westwards, knowing that we would not be safe until dark – the day seemed very long. This time it was clear that there was no hope of getting *Pennland* going again, so she abandoned ship and we picked up the survivors. Mercifully, she had as yet no troops on board as we had never reached the loading port. There had been few losses among the crew who were phlegmatic Dutch and included some pretty nurses. In one of the later alarms, Jon Walley was reputed gallantly to have flung one of these on the deck and bravely covered her with his far from small body. She was surprised, especially as the noise didn't come from a bomb at all. When all were rescued, we turned our attention to the hulk. It isn't every day that a gunnery control officer gets to shoot holes in a big liner at point-blank range. We got lots of shells into her but, embarrassingly, she wouldn't sink. At last making several holes in her waterline, she slowly keeled over and disappeared. We had not wanted to waste a good torpedo on her; one never knew whether the Italian fleet might not show up. Had they done so they might have had a field day because our battle fleet had to remain in Alexandria, all screening destroyers being needed for the evacuation. Luckily, Matapan had cooled what ardour they had.

It was now too late to catch up with the Megara convoy, so we returned to Suda, landed the survivors, and fuelled again early on the 25th. An hour later, we were off again, this time to join another evacuation convoy going to Nauplia and Tolon. This convoy turned out to be the most ill-fated of them all. We joined them a little after 0900. It consisted of *Glenearn, Slamat, Khedive, Ismail* and *Ulster Prince*, escorted by the a-a cruiser, we, *Diamond, Wryneck* and *Hotspur*. All day we plodded northwards, watching the sun climb to its zenith, and sink – much too slowly. There were various attacks, none particularly effective until quite late in the evening just when we were beginning to feel that we might get through the day.

This attack by Ju.87s was well carried out. A large bomb hit the *Glenearn*, wrecking her steering gear and filling her with 7,000 tons of water. She was a particularly valuable ship, being one of three 'Glen' ships fitted with landing craft and sent to the Mediterranean to carry out an invasion of Rhodes – this, in happier times, weeks earlier. Now she was the very thing for an evacuation, and must be saved. But when we were the ones detailed to tow her back to Crete, our hearts sank a little. There were still a couple of hours of daylight in front of us. The prospect of being sitting ducks at slow speed for the next wave of dive-bombers did not please. But the job of getting the monster in tow fully occupied my thoughts. Once again, Florrie on the quarterdeck was a tower of strength.

Things did not go well because *Glenearn*'s rudder was jammed in a hardover position and she could not move it. Thus every time we got the tow under way, she merely started turning and in doing so pulled our stern round so that we ended up pointing in her direction, and no amount of juggling with the engines would help. She must by now have weighed some 20,000 tons, but did not seem to be sinking any further. I remember her Captain Hill, an old-timer recalled from retirement, sitting on his bridge as calm as could be, handing out cigars when we found ourselves alongside her. Twice our tow parted, until we had no more suitable wire available. The navigator's notebook reads, 'Deadlock with tow. *Glenearn* swings to starboard.' At midnight, the last chance. *Glenearn* had a very large five and a half inch wire, which had to be led out of her small and cluttered forecastle. Normally under these conditions, Murphy's Law prevails: if something can get caught up, it will; and at the worst possible time. But *Griffin* was lucky again. The wire ran out sweetly, we were able to connect it to a length of cable, and this time it held. By now *Glenearn* had succeeded in getting her rudder a little straighter, so we were able to get her going, turning very gradually southward towards Crete at eight knots. This embarrassing position is known in minesweeping circles, for obvious reasons, as 'going doggo'.

At dawn, there was the inevitable Ju.88 shadowing and we expected the worst. Miraculously, no attack developed.

Our 'friends' must have been busy elsewhere, as we later knew. For most of the day we crept southwards, still on tenterhooks. We sighted *Ajax* at one stage, and *Perth*, *Orion* and destroyers at another, but they were busy with their own affairs. At last at 1530 or so we got her into Kissamo Bay at the west end of Crete, and the sloop *Grimsby* took her over from us. She eventually reached Alexandria after more bombing near Gavdo Island.

Diamond and *Wryneck*

As soon as we were free, it was into Suda Bay, but only for twenty minutes. Nothing had been heard of *Diamond* or *Wryneck* and it was almost certain that they had been sunk so back we went at twenty-five knots towards Nauplia, the original destination of the convoy. We know now that we had been lucky to stay with *Glenearn*. Everything had gone wrong at Nauplia. *Ulster Prince* had been bombed, set on fire and run aground, forming a beacon for further attacks. The other big ships could not get in, so the destroyers had to ferry troops out to them. This all took valuable time and, to cap it all, *Slamat* was unpardonably slow in getting under way. At daylight the whole remaining convoy was only a few miles on the way home. Then *Slamat* was sunk, *Diamond* and *Wryneck* had to pick up many hundreds of soldiers, and were proceeding, heavily loaded, at full speed when they too were overwhelmed by an unseen attack out of the sun, and sunk.

As we hurried northward during the rest of the night, we received orders to search for survivors but not to linger after dawn. Time went on, and nothing was seen or heard, then at 0200 we heard shouts and found two Carley floats with a few survivors from *Wryneck*. That was all. Knowing that *Diamond* could not have been very far away when she was sunk, we searched around until just before dawn. It was high time to leave. Then, just before 0600 we sighted two more floats with oil-covered men on them. Of course, it took quite a while to pick them up. They had been exhausted when sunk, and were now in the last stages. Each time we got a few inboard and were ready to depart, we came upon a few more – pathetic little groups of those who had lasted the day and night. Johnny now had a difficult decision: should we obey instructions, or should we risk losing the survivors, and ourselves, and search further in hopes of finding a few more. We stayed on another hour, biting our fingernails until there really appeared to be no hope of finding any more. Then turned and fled for the comparative safety of Suda Bay, all the while gazing yet again into the mounting sun. To me the saddest thing was the loss of my term-mate John Marshall, my opposite number in the *Diamond*. Although one of her boats was later found to have reached a Greek island, he was not in it. We had picked up less than 50 men out of about 900 in the three ships.

Monemvasia

We had four hours in harbour after landing the survivors, interrupted as usual by air-raid warnings. All of us were by now short of sleep, but somehow one managed to keep going for the next operation, which was to go to Monemvasia (in happier times a source of some of the better, non-resinous Greek wines) to evacuate those soldiers who had managed to get so far south.

It was not a long passage from Crete and we arrived after dark having, on the way, carried out a burial service for some who did not survive the last rescue. I read the service at dusk and committed the dead to the deep under the white ensign; a most moving moment. It was only a little later, to my horror, that the chief boatswain's mate found one more hidden under a pile of oily rags and clothing. I did not feel that I could get the ship's company out again and so, saying a quiet prayer, we sent him to join the others.

The evacuation at Monemvasia went quite well. This time it was destroyers and cruisers only. There were some primitive landing craft available, making the work much easier as we could not get alongside. A bit of light relief occurred when one boat came alongside crammed with men in khaki. We got them inboard and hustled them forward into the mess decks to make room for more. One tall figure with a bit of a limp was inclined to make trouble, but he was grasped by the arm ('you're all right now, soldier') and led forward until he made it very clear that he was not a 'soldier' but Rear Admiral Tom Baillie-Grohman, the flag officer in charge of the whole Greek evacuation. We placated him but he insisted on 'taking charge' and was really rather a nuisance until he fell backwards in the darkness into an open gun well and balanced up his limp thereafter. I was glad when he transferred to the cruiser *Ajax* as being more fitting to his standing and, admittedly, possessed of better communications. We were sorry not to be the ones to get the famous General Freyberg, who was somewhere there in the dark.

One good thing about these later evacuations was that, being close to our base, we operated at night. The German air force only operated by day so we were pretty safe. Nor did we have any trouble with submarines or the Italian surface fleet who must have been still smarting after Matapan. So all went well this time and we delivered a good quota of soldiers – Australians and New Zealanders, a splendid looking bunch – to Crete where further troubles lay ahead for them.

Rover

For us it was almost the end. We were not in on the last night at Kalamata as we were given yet another towing job. This time we had to get the submarine *Rover* to Alexandria. She had been near-missed and her engines were out of action. Once again, towing was not an attractive occupation because one could not take avoiding action, normally our best hope when attacked. So it was important not to be spotted. It was about now that Johnny cleared lower deck and had us all round the 3" a-a gun (which was manned) and held a short prayer service. I for one felt better for it. And, indeed, it worked!

While we secured the tow there was a massive attack on the harbour by Ju.88s but after that things were quiet. We got her going nicely and cast well out to the westward to get away from the normal Crete-Alexandria track. We had a big white bow wave painted on the stern, and tried to look as though we had no connection with the conning tower astern. Anyhow we had no problems, arriving off Alexandria on 1 May to find the harbour closed due to mines. Eventually the tow was passed to the net layer *Protector* and we got in at 1930 that evening. The notebook merely reads, 'at last'.

I was interested to read, years later, an obituary in *The Times*, which had the following: '... the submarine was towed by the destroyer *Griffin* to Alexandria. Miraculously both ships survived the tow, but as no one in the Royal Navy would admit to having sanctioned such a risky adventure, little mention was made of the episode.' An over-dramatization, I think.

Next day we received a most rare and welcome signal from ABC commending us on our efforts. Later, he came on board. Not one to be lavish with praise, he never forgot what we were up against.

Years later J. L-B told me that the staff had arranged for a small tug to tow *Rover* at 4 or 5 knots, and we were to escort them along the shortest Crete-Alexandria route. Johnny thought this would be suicide and refused to do it that way. Instead, we towed her ourselves at 12 to 15 knots and kept well to the westward of 'bomb alley'. Once again, we had reason to be grateful for Johnny's independence and common sense.

Tiger

We actually got four clear days and nights in Alexandria to recuperate. The C-in-C himself had 'hoped for a respite', noting 'signs of strain among destroyer crews'. But another urgent commitment cropped up. The army had such a desperate need for tanks that the Admiralty, prodded by Churchill, had decided to risk sending a fast five-ship convoy straight through the Mediterranean instead of around the Cape. The operation was called Tiger.

We left Alexandria on the morning of 6 May with the whole fleet, after some delay due to mines, in the entrance. En route to Malta we refuelled from *Breconshire* and apart from the usual warnings no attack of any kind developed. In the most vulnerable area around Malta we were favoured, for a change, with a lot of fog and very low cloud, so the enemy never found us. We picked up the four merchant ships, which had got past Malta, together with the battleship *Queen Elizabeth* and the cruisers *Fiji* and *Naiad*, and made off back to Alexandria. We could have done with another aircraft carrier.

The enemy eventually found us too late for attack by day on the 10th. But that night there was a brilliant full moon and we were subjected to much bombing by aircraft, which came in one at a time. Although one felt rather naked in the moonlight, perhaps we were not so visible as we thought. The fleet put up a spectacular barrage. No one was hit and we were back in Alexandria on the 12th. Altogether the operation was a great and somewhat unexpected success for which I am sure the army must have been most grateful. Doubtless Churchill thought 'I told you so' – but we had been lucky with the weather.

Crete

This time there were five clear days in harbour before the next item on the programme, which was obviously going to be a German assault on Crete. I have little recollection of what we did, except sleep and generally clean up. The engine room department had much to do, for by now the ship was beginning to feel the effects of twenty-two months hard steaming during which time we must have covered about 200,000 miles without major refit.

The expected summons came on 18 May, when we sailed with Admiral Rawlings and the battleships. The *Formidable* did not come as she was now down to four serviceable aircraft. So no air cover could be expected. We set off to a position to the west of Crete to await the invasion. There were the usual shadowers, air raid warnings and sporadic attacks. Destroyers refuelled in turn, we from *Valiant*. The sun rose and set in a cloudless sky and one counted the hours to dark. I remember being in two watches – either in the director tower for gunnery control or waiting in the chart house nearby, reading *Death in the Afternoon*, an appropriate title, about bullfighting, also appropriate for Crete.

On the 20th the invasion began with the dropping of an airborne division of paratroops around Canea, preceded by heavy bombing of our army's defensive positions. On this day we were left reasonably well alone as presumably our main opponents, Fliegerkorps VIII (incidentally commanded by a General von Richthofen, a cousin of the Red Baron) were fully occupied. But next day things warmed up, culminating in a heavy attack in the evening after waves of it all day. One wondered how long the ammunition would last. Just before dusk it was heartening to see the wing shot off one Ju.87 as he circled above before his dive. He turned over and over, crashing into the sea with a mighty splash. I was reminded of Icarus, and felt glad to be fighting in these classical waters. I hoped the Gods would be on our side.

That night we were formed into Force B with our sister *Greyhound* and the cruisers *Gloucester* and *Fiji*, and entered the Aegean past Antikithera to look for the German sea invasion forces. Clearly it was going to be a sticky night and day. Indeed, twenty-four hours later we were the only ship in the force still afloat. I had the middle watch and turned in early to get some sleep, but it wouldn't come. I think that this time I was really frightened and said a number of prayers. At midnight I was up and on watch. Shortly afterwards we went to action stations. It would have been grand to have stumbled on one of the enemy's little convoys, as did our opposite numbers at the other end of Crete; they demolished them.

We found nothing, and at least no enemy landed from the sea at our end. But at dawn we were still well inside the Aegean without air support of any kind. Sure enough a little after 0600 the imperturbable A.B. Morgan, our best lookout, saw the first lot. He had a maddeningly deliberate way of reporting: 'six – eight – ten – sixteen – no, twenty aircraft bearing green 140, sir. Look like Junkers 87s.' He sounded as though this were a fleet exercise. The Stukas kept coming our way, climbing and eventually circling like hawks on a thermal. Then down in groups of three, one after the other, dividing their attentions among all four ships. It was a classic attack, technically interesting, physically terrifying and, actually, ineffectual. Somehow, they missed us all as we weaved at full speed and the cruisers put up plenty of flak. We popped off with our 3" museum piece, and our .5" machine guns did their best with their antediluvian control system. They deserved better luck as one could see holes appearing in the aircraft, but little bullets like that weren't much use unless they hit the pilot in a painful place. By now we were steaming westwards on our way out of the 'trap' at high speed to join the battleships beyond Kithera. The next attack came at 0800. It hadn't taken them long to return. Their bases can only have been a few miles away.

Again they scored no hits and not long after we thankfully sighted the mastheads of the battle fleet, which had moved in to give us support. There was safety in numbers, like schools of sardines. Another of the night's detached forces had already rejoined, having had the satisfaction of annihilating a convoy headed for western Crete. *Ajax* had rammed one of them and was reputed to be steaming around with a German soldier with a fixed bayonet stuck to her stern. By the time the next wave came over at 0900 we were in company and felt a little better. But there was still a long day ahead and as it went on the battle became more continuous. It appeared that the Germans were attacking, returning to base, refuelling and bombing up, then coming back to the fray without waiting for whole squadrons to assemble. As a result, there was really no letup. The big ships started to conserve ammunition so their barrages were rather less effective. At about 1300 we were joined by yet another of the night forces, this one under Admiral King who took over command, being senior to Admiral Rawlings. Their experience had been worse, if anything, than ours. *Carlisle* had been hit on the bridge and her captain killed. *Naiad* had thirty-six near misses in ten minutes. Sadly, they had sighted a convoy bound for Canea but due to the heaviness of air attack did not pursue it when it turned back. ABC later said that they should have gone after it anyway, but it is doubtful whether, if they had, any of them would have survived.

No sooner had we all assembled than a lone Messerschmitt 109 glided out of some low cloud, of which there was a little about, and hit the *Warspite* amidships with a large bomb. It was by no means the first or the last time that the grand old lady had been hit in her splendid career. She had about 100 casualties and, emitting a great cloud of smoke, looked a good deal more stricken than she actually was. It was a bad moment, but before long she had things under control and the day went on. Halfway now.

Then a serious mistake was made. *Greyhound* was detached to sink a caique near Antikithera. Any one of us could have foretold her fate. On the way to rejoin, still alone, she was set upon and sunk by eight Ju.87s. About 100 men got away in rafts and a whaler. While they were in the water, they were machine-gunned. Her first lieutenant, Robert Scott, was killed, and Henry Trefusis, recently lent from us, was one of the survivors of the whaler, buried under a heap of dead. Poor old *Greyhound* was the last of our flotilla apart from ourselves. It could so easily have been *Griffin*. We were still a 'lucky ship'. After this performance we would not rescue the crews of downed German aircraft.

Ten minutes later, out on the screen, we received some attention. The bombs missed but the Stuka machine-gunned us on the way down, wounding two men at the back of the bridge. And so it went on until at last the sun went down on what had been, for me at any rate, the worst day of the war. Unfortunately there were other repercussions from *Greyhound*'s loss. *Kandahar* and *Kingston* were detached in their turn to pick up survivors, among them *Greyhound*'s Captain Marshall à-Deane, who that evening lost his life trying to rescue others. The cruisers *Gloucester* and *Fiji*, our companions of last night, were also detached to give support. But they were both low in ammunition and by the end of the day were both sunk with heavy loss of life. *Fiji* had been reduced to firing practice ammunition and was hit in the last attack before dark. So much for Force B, of which we were the only survivors. The lesson of it all, which should have been known already, was: stick together.

That night we fell out from action stations and got a few hours sleep. Early next morning, to our surprise, the whole force headed south for Alexandria. It appeared that the C-in-C had ordered this, thinking that the battleships, too, were out of ammunition. Otherwise, doubtless, we should have stayed on. It was on this day that not far away, Mountbatten was sunk in the *Kelly* with the *Kashmir*. *Kipling* managed to bring the survivors home. On our own way home, no attacks developed and we entered Alexandria early on 24 May, utterly exhausted.

And here we stayed for two weeks while the rest of the cruisers and destroyers went back for the evacuation. Our engines had given up the ghost and we had to go alongside the repair ship *Resource* (also known as the despair ship Remorse). The tribulations of the evacuation have been well described by Hugh Hodgkinson, the first lieutenant of our chummy ship *Hotspur* in his book *Before the Tide Turned*, written in 1941 after he had been invalided home. In a way one felt badly to see the others return with varying degrees of damage and exhaustion. But one lived for the day and we tried to make the most of it.

Alexandria Again

Alexandria, though not a very satisfactory naval base, was a superb place to go ashore. The situation was unusual in that Egypt was not technically at war. We had the treaty right to use the harbours and the duty to defend the frontiers. Thus, although the Germans and Italians came over at night to try to bomb the fleet, they weren't supposed to bomb the cities so, on the whole, Alexandria was barely touched. The raids on the harbour were nothing much to worry about, although the *Decoy* once got a bomb (which didn't explode) right through her wardroom. I sat in my cabin on several occasions with John Somerville from *Hero* listening to music on the moonlight nights when they came over. One was pretty safe and left the action to the army and the big ships. There was one night when, lying alongside one of the quays to load up for Tobruk, we saw a land mine on the end of a parachute land not far away. Within minutes, the shadowy figures of Egyptians had removed the parachute and vanished. The mine was rendered safe by the military.

I developed quite a soft spot for the Egyptians who had a rather horrible sense of humour, usually expressed with a ghastly toothless grin. At one time before the war we used to sit at a bar in the open air and a dreadful Arab would pass quietly below, trying to sell bunches of overpoweringly sweet-smelling gardenias. In a deep voice: 'Lovely flowers, too, too divine.' They had a genius for imitating OK English accents. On another occasion, an infuriated major shouted at an obstructive Egyptian who was loading stores in the wrong place. The 'gyppo' smiled sweetly at the major and assumed a cockney accent. 'Up your fat arse,' he said. And I heard that the famous Fitzroy McLean, then a brigadier based in Cairo, was described by his suffragi as follows: 'BUGADDEER very good man. By and by him cactchit scissors.' (For the uninitiated, this refers to the crossed swords on a major general's shoulder badges).

Ashore, nothing was wanting. Food, drink, clothes, petrol, everything was as in peacetime. Alexandria was full of uniforms; sailors, soldiers and airmen on leave of many nationalities. Although practically nothing has survived above ground of its ancient history, I always found the city to be reeking of it, in particular the foundations of the Pharos just under the eastern harbour. Perhaps it was fanciful to feel the presence of Alexander (my namesake?), Julius Caesar, Antony, Cleopatra, and the great library. But I did and I believe that it gave me strength.

Apart from all that, the so-called 'fleshpots' were unrivalled. Bars, restaurants, shops, and clubs abounded, full of good things and cosmopolitan clientele. One felt that spies abounded and wondered how many of the population would actually welcome the enemy. We used to frequent a particular bar whose name I forget, but whose barman – Kypros – I do not. Here one had free caviar with one's drinks before going on to Pastroudis, the Ritz or the Union Club for dinner. The latter had excellent onion soup and sole chasseur. A Dutchman, on his way home from the East Indies, was reputed to have gone ashore to dine there, and stayed for the rest of his life. Later in the evenings, we haunted the Monseigneur where there were cabarets and dancing. Finally, there was Mary's House, a high-class brothel that need not be used as such but provided, on the ground floor, food and drink; one could borrow money from Mary if temporarily embarrassed. Later in the war, a bomb fell there and certain officers, caught upstairs, were said to have been killed in action. Mary herself, no mean person, travelled around Alexandria in a big fur coat and a Mercedes convertible, known to all.

One evening, Captain (D) 7th Destroyer Flotilla, Steve Arliss, whose parents had given him the unfortunate initials S.H.T., was seen sitting with a lovely lady who had her arm around him, fingering his medal ribbons and was heard to murmur, 'Oh Stevie, what a brave man you are.' This endeared him to all of us.

There was also the Sporting Club where one could play tennis, squash or watch the plump Greek ladies with lovely skins busy filling themselves with rich sticky cakes. The contrast between time ashore and time at sea was really ludicrous. A few people left suitcases ashore, ready packed with civilian clothes so that if sunk they could step straight into them. I didn't do this. On the whole we drank a great deal and played the fool a lot, often with some agreeable survivors of the desert tank battles. Playing the fool consisted on occasion of innocent pastimes like trying to extract large potted palm trees from nightclubs and getting them back on board. The most dangerous of these was an occasion when, with some Australians, it was thought a good idea to remove the front wheels from an Egyptian taxi whose driver was charging too much. We vanished just in time before the crowd arrived.

There wasn't much time or inclination for womanizing although we had some nice parties at expatriates' private houses with a little amateur song and dance group. There were no Wrens in those days. I think the biggest contrast of all happened a little later when we were in the Gabbari dock and at extended notice for sea. I flew by Misr Airlines up to Cairo and spent a weekend with an Egyptian family called Adda. Charles, a Cairo lawyer, was a brother of an old friend in England who was a rather wealthy cotton broker. Their apartment was to me something out of the *Arabian Nights*. Sudanese servants, black as your hat, with white jelabiyas and red sashes. We dined by candlelight on the roof, not a breath of wind stirring, the stars brilliant and close above. I did my tour of the Pyramids, the Sphinx of course, Shepherd's Hotel. Then back to the bottom of a dock.

There was so much to do and see ashore in the brief breaks that one did not want to waste any time. As a result, I used to come back on board very late and rarely caught up on sleep. To add to that problem, on the evenings when we were at short notice and didn't go ashore, Johnny would hold court over glasses of port until early hours in the morning. Or we would sing the usual ribald songs of which we had a repertoire to be proud (depending on your point of view). Only Clifford (Button) Studd had the strength of mind to break off early sometimes with the words, 'I have something important to attend to.'

A few changes had occurred in the wardroom. Dick Coulton went to *Neptune* where he was lost. Mike Hennell had arrived early in the New Year to meet an agreeable fate in the Monseigneur, of which more in its place. Ian Paterson, a very young RNVR sub and specialist in women, left the backs of some of our charts covered with only competent sketches of lovely young ladies, scantily clad. Our splendid West Country ship's company remained, so far virtually untouched, as the drafting people's claws hadn't yet reached us. This must have had some influence on our survival. I have only encountered one in recent years – 'Lofty' Coning, our gunner's mate who ended up as I did in British Columbia – a great character.

So administrative work wasn't too demanding which was just as well. But the ship had to be kept clean, painted and repaired. Examination for higher rating must go on, request men and defaulters seen, gunnery and other drills continued and lists of stores and armament supplies kept up to date. This last task fell behind in my case, I must confess. I couldn't find the energy to pursue what might be a completely wasted effort at any time.

I look back on Alexandria with fondness, but dare not go back there.

One of the things which tended to keep up morale was our collection of live things. This started, of course, with Jamie, the captain's bull terrier who didn't like loud noises or late nights but got plenty of both. Then, when a gully-gully-man came on board doing tricks with chicks, we bought some off him and kept them in the spud locker; the procedure being that if you wanted a fresh egg, very small, you paid for it with a bar of 'nutty'. The supply petty officer got half as a perk for looking after the livestock and the chicken got half for producing the egg. On one of our trips to Aden, the Maltese mess man returned with some live pigeons for a stew. But we hadn't the heart to kill them, so some spaces were cleared among the less used flag lockers on the signal deck, and the pigeons survived there for many weeks. The biggest one, Blackie, was brought down to the top of the wardroom hatch, at a given signal, whenever we had a party. He was then let loose to flutter down into the wardroom to light on the head of some startled guest. Alas, one by one the pigeons failed to return when flying too far from the ship at sea. Then we got a duck. On one occasion we were visited by the Egyptian Minister of Information, Lufti Bey, a charming gentleman in a nice grey suit and a tarbush. Regrettably, it was after a good lunch, and he was shown far too little of our armaments and far too much of our livestock, being at last presented with an egg, which he carried down to the boat gingerly and rather incredulously. Later on, we got a monkey, a turtle, a lemur, and a chameleon. The latter lived in the wardroom and was supposed to catch flies with its long tongue. But it sat on a lampshade all day and didn't even change colour much.

Syria

By the end of the Crete evacuation, the Mediterranean fleet was much reduced and there were less than twenty destroyers operational. No one quite knew what the next call would be, and when it came it caused some surprise. The Germans had been infiltrating Syria and Iraq, and the French in Syria were cooperating, so it was necessary to invade that country to protect our flank and the oilfields behind it. This time it was not necessary to transport the army by sea, and our role was to support their advance up the coast from Palestine. As usual, we had little or no air support – indeed at one stage we were bombed by our own aircraft – Blenheims – who thought we were French, or something. But this time there was something to shoot at other than German aircraft.

We sailed from Alexandria on 9 June 1941 with *Jaguar*, *Stuart* and *Defender* and were soon off Haifa. The rest of the month was spent operating from there, moving gradually northwards as the army advanced. We started our bombardments off the ancient port of Sidon (which has since suffered many more), the target being the coast road along which the French, who were fighting hard, ran their supplies. This was rather fun. We closed in as near as we could, there being no mines that we knew of, and let fly at lorries and the occasional tank. On one occasion a small tank or armoured car stopped with part of it showing round the corner of a dilapidated farmhouse. 'Number One,' said the bridge. 'Do you see the tank?' 'Yes.' 'Then hit it, but don't hit the house.' 'Aye aye, sir.' Off went B gun, and, of course, hit the house from which emerged some enraged Arabs who shook their fists at us. The tank crew bailed out and ran up the hill.

On another occasion, further up the coast at Damour, all the destroyers and a couple of cruisers clobbered a big banana plantation where the French were dug in and holding up the Australians. We cleared them out nicely in a morning.[11] The French had no means of hitting us from the shore, so it was all relatively carefree. On several days the Ju.88s came over a long way from Rhodes and had a shot at us, but without effect.

A bigger menace were two very large and fast French destroyers based in Beirut, the *Valmy* and the *Guépard*. They had 5" guns and fired shells, which made coloured bursts – red, or green to distinguish which fall of shot belonged to which ship. Just before we arrived the *Janus* was hit by a green one, which stopped her and dyed her captain's (John Tothill) beard green, after which he was known as 'Fungus 14' (we now belonged to the 14th Destroyer Flotilla).

The Frenchmen used to dash out of Beirut, interrupt our bombardment, and then retire behind their coastal batteries before our covering cruisers could get them. On 16 June at dawn we had a taste of these fellows who straddled us nicely but did not score a hit. It was an uncomfortable moment but didn't last long. Appropriately, the headland off which this skirmish occurred was named 'Ras am Shit', but we never claimed the battle honour. That afternoon a French submarine fired a couple of torpedoes at us, but Signalman Carkett redeemed his normal troublesome career by spotting them in good time. The day before this we had another visitation by Ju.88s, which damaged both *Isis* and *Ilex* quite seriously. They eventually got away for nice long refits.

All in all, this month was an enjoyable picnic. Haifa turned out to be a most entertaining base apart from some night air raids which didn't bother us much. The swimming was superb. I remember particularly an afternoon at Athlit where the remains of a Crusader castle lay right on the shoreline. I even went on a bus trip with a party of sailors, accompanied by the Reverend Sherlock (known as Shylock the flotilla chaplain, temporarily with us) to Nazareth, Cana and the Sea of Galilee. Nazareth proved to be a scruffy, Arab town full of touts. Cana was not much better. There, they produced the 'genuine' jars in which our Lord turned water into wine! In neither of these did I feel any sense of our Lord. But looking down on the Sea of Galilee moved me immensely. There was no one about at all, and among the wild flowers one could feel that nothing had changed in a thousand years. Back via the Vale of Armageddon (were we experiencing it?), a ride only spoiled for the Reverend by the number of sailors who wanted to stop the bus at places of no religious significance. They had had a lot of beer in Nazareth.

The contrast, even then, between the derelict Arab countryside and the orderly, flourishing Jewish settlement was most marked. But I retained a sympathetic feeling for the displaced Arabs with their ramshackle flocks. A land flowing with milk and honey (in parts).

Each day, carts with those very items drew up alongside, a pleasant change from tinned 'Carnation'. Another pleasant surprise was the arrival on board of an official who asked whether the wardroom would like to buy, at a nominal price, a consignment of Chianti, destined for the Duke of Aosta, Viceroy of Abyssinia, but seized when Italy came into the war. We took as much as we could stow and for months drank it, making a substantial profit for the wine fund at a penny a glass. It was no ordinary wine.

Nightlife was fun in Haifa, too. 'Pross' and other excellent clubs provided food, drink, music, and dancing. Phil May and I (he from the submarine *Parthian*, sole survivor of my term seven submariners) had a lot of amusement playing the double bass with a Yugoslav band. On 30 June, Johnny got his brass hat and we had an evening even more riotous than usual when an infuriated artiste chased the new commander out of her dressing room just as he was putting on some particularly attractive filmy clothing of hers. But we never got to Beirut, to my regret, having nightly seen those beckoning lights getting closer as we edged up the coast. An armistice was signed on 11 July and we returned to Alexandria to await developments.

The Tobruk Run

At this point, my series of navigator's notebooks (which I appropriated much later when we paid off) runs out and I rely on memory and the history books for dates and details. Of course the major event of this period was the German invasion of Russia on 22 June 1941. This must have eased the weight of air attack, which otherwise we would have felt. Even so, there seemed to be plenty of Ju.87s and 88s in the desert area. And it was here that we were now to be mainly occupied. The German army was on the Egyptian border, and the port of Tobruk, 300 miles from Alexandria, had been bypassed. It had been besieged since 11 April. Various inshore flotillas, including the valiant Australian destroyers and fast minelayers were employed on what was known as the 'Bread Run' or 'Beef and Spud Run'.

We did many of these in the next three months, and they fell into a pattern. You went alongside one of the quays to load up with all kinds of stores – vegetables, ammunition, beer, water, meat – all the things the army puts in its stomach and marches on. Loading was done by Gyppy labour and they dropped marrows and watermelons everywhere. A smell of mashed vegetables still brings back the memory. Then a group – normally one fast minelayer and four destroyers – would leave Alexandria so that you were still under fighter cover (we had some in the desert by now) until dark. Then it was full speed, zigzagging frequently to avoid the U-boats, until about 2330 when you turned towards the coast, trying to find the entrance. It was, of course, heavily mined, and a channel was kept open by some very brave sweepers who hid alongside the many wrecks by day. The channel was marked by a green light, which hadn't much visibility. Once you spotted it, you could steam in on a line of bearing, hoping that the Germans hadn't set up their own green light leading you to the minefields. You then made your way into the harbour, which was littered with wrecks, some of which could be used to unload stores. You had an absolute maximum of 45 minutes to get all 50 tons of stuff offloaded down wooden chutes, cast off and get out at full speed to be under the fighter umbrella at dawn. If you got caught it was probably curtains. To add to the incentive, a big gun called Bardia Bill would lob shells onto the harbour from outside the perimeter. If you had time, you could watch the Very lights and occasional firing along the trenches around the besieged area. It was like a spectator's look at World War I.

A further complication came about when it became necessary to withdraw the Australian division who had done hard fighting and were needed at home to face the Japanese threat. They were to be replaced by the Polish division who were, as always, anxious to fight. So this meant embarking, in addition to the stores, some 300 Poles, all of whom were perfectly disciplined and sat or lay about quietly throughout the trip. On arrival, they got out quickly enough but it was a problem to get the Aussies moving. They were not going to hurry for anyone, but the last few did get a sort of shuffle going when we started to cast off. All this in the pitch darkness because the runs were not feasible in moonlight. We got quite good at it after a while. The Aussies remained a rather wild bunch, messy too, for those who had to clear up after them. I suppose they were used to throwing empty cans away underfoot in the desert. On arrival in Alexandria harbour with one lot, I was startled by a fusillade of musketry. Another air raid? Shooting traitors? No, just a few soldiers aiming at seagulls on a buoy. But they, along with a number of Sikhs and Gurkhas (who were reputed to have some German ears) were fine warriors.

We were at action stations all night on these runs, but one could doze off from time to time. I, in my director tower, was not uncomfortable. There were various alarms, the most startling of which was a U-boat on the surface, which passed a few yards down our starboard side. Each of us was too close to do anything and passing too fast – 30 knots for us and 10 for him. We couldn't stop to hunt and dared not write ourselves off by ramming him, so we waved and went our separate ways.

Occasionally we were bothered by Italian Savoia torpedo bombers, affectionately known as Ferdinand and Isabel, but we were going too fast for them to achieve anything. A Ju.88 (Dan the Regular Man), used to appear at 4 pm. But, as so often on our runs, we were lucky. Some weren't, however. The minelayer *Latona* was set on fire one evening and sunk; *Defender*, *Waterhen*, *Grimsby* (which had taken over the tow of *Glenearn* from us in Greece), and *Auckland* were all sunk between Alexandria and Tobruk. I also remember some very nervous officers from a little high-octane petrol tanker called the *Pass of Balmaha*, which used to do unescorted runs at about ten knots. It seemed suicidal, and indeed, it was. One day she exploded in a ball of fire, and nothing remained. I don't know whether her crew ever received any recognition.

On another of the runs, while we were under the fighter umbrella, the pilot of one of our fighters was shot down and had to bale out. We went to pick him up. We came nicely up to him as he swam in the water and were about to lift him aboard when he disappeared from view under the ship. It turned out that he had been unable to release his parachute, which trailed below him to get sucked down into our condenser inlets. After what seemed a long time, miraculously the pilot came up the other side; one of the rare cases of an airman being keelhauled. He was a Rhodesian and a very nice fellow. He bore no ill will, recovered surprisingly quickly and went back to the desert for more.

On Trafalgar Day, 21 October, we were given the task of rescuing the ex-China river gunboat *Gnat* off Bardia. She had been torpedoed by a U-boat – a subtle feat of depth estimation, as those gunboats only drew a couple of feet. As a result, her bows were blown right off, leaving her a more or less oblong shape. The survivors were rather inclined to abandon ship when we arrived, but as she was floating like a cork, Johnny tactfully indicated that he would pick them up when she had sunk. So we got a towing wire on board and towed her diamond fashion by one corner. *Jaguar* came and circled round us to keep the U-boat away and we had excellent fighter protection all the way home. At one stage, it was proposed that *Gnat's* rear end should be grafted onto the bows of the *Cricket*, with a resultant hybrid *Gnacket*, but nothing came of it.

On one night in Tobruk, going alongside a wreck to unload, we struck our stern against a projecting part of the wreck. This bent our 'nose' and the result was a fine bow wave of spray as we gathered speed. As we already had a false bow wave painted there, it did no harm, though it was a little embarrassing until it was straightened out at the next docking. Actually, Johnny was a master ship-handler and it was seldom that our berthing parties had to do more than hand over the lines.

One other run sticks in my memory. After a very late night ashore at our usual spots, we left harbour early in the morning and headed at high speed into a nasty rough sea. I had the duty of supervising 'up spirits', which entailed going down into a small compartment below the stoker's mess deck and watching the coxswain pumping rum up from a fresh cask. A combination of rum fumes, a hangover and express-left effect [sic] made me feel really ill and I had to fight an overpowering need to be seasick, in front of the assembled mess men. I only just made it.

Between runs to Tobruk we occasionally went out with the fleet – now three old battleships and a handful of cruisers. ABC was always champing at the bit, but the big ships were now normally condemned to spend most of their time in harbour because the destroyers were all too busy on other duties to provide a screen – or even to keep in practice at anti-submarine work. The idea of these 'club runs' with the fleet was usually to make the enemy think we were either supplying Malta or meeting a through convoy to Malta from the east, but we hoped we could take some pressure off Force H from Gibraltar.

On one occasion in September 1941 we went to sea for exercises with our leader, the *Jervis*, who took as a passenger Admiral Wells (retired) the Director General, Ports and Lights. In this Egyptian capacity, he always wore a red tarbush. The press later headlined the item: 'BLUE-EYED EGYPTIAN ADMIRAL REVIEWS BRITAIN'S CRACK FLOTILLA'.

At the end of October 1941, we at last got a substantial break and entered Gabbari Dock for a refit. It was on this occasion that I managed to get up to Cairo. It was pretty unpleasant in the dock, especially when we were engulfed in a 'hamseen' or sandstorm, which penetrated every crevice, filled the ship with small flies and made it hard to breathe.

Some substantial alterations were made to the ship: in particular – oh joy! – we were fitted with two 20-millimetre Oerlikon guns, one on either side of the bridge. At last, after two years, we would be able to shoot back at those maddening dive-bombers. To compensate for the extra weight our after funnel was cut down, which rather spoiled our looks. We also received a most primitive form of radar, which gave some small warning of large metal objects encountered at sea. But one had to turn the ship to get a proper bearing, and the set never worked very well. The sailors' drying room was used to house the equipment, adding to their discomforts resulting from the extra crew to man these new items.

New Faces

It was during this refit that we lost Johnny Lee-Barber, who was recalled to England having had such an exceptionally arduous command during which he had collected two DSOs and deserved more. We were, of course, sad to see him go, and the ship's company dance which bid him farewell was an emotional occasion. It was also the end of our peacetime crew, for at the same time a large proportion of it was relieved to go home and man new ships. Johnny and most of our best men went home round the Cape. I felt rather forlorn and wondered how long I would stay. It turned out to be more than a year. Meanwhile the reliefs we received were of the worst; fellows who had been kicking around Alexandria as spare numbers; many survivors of sunken ships, feeling that they should be going home too; and a nasty nucleus of troublemakers from the detention quarters.

Captain (D)

No sooner had we 'welcomed' this lot aboard than another startling change occurred. Instead of a straight relief for J. L-B., we found we were to house Captain (D), Second Destroyer Flotilla, Hugh Nicolson and his staff. I was to stay on as first lieutenant and once again found myself vastly junior to be executive officer of a leader.

All the staff was greatly senior to me and didn't mind showing it. With a couple of exceptions, I didn't care for them at all, and found 'Nick' rather selfish and unapproachable, especially in comparison with George Creasy and Philip Mack.

The additional staff and communications ratings also made life on board cramped and uncomfortable both for officers and men. But no expense was spared in providing an oval mahogany table for the wardroom. I gloomily watched it taking shape, polished daily for hours by a one-eyed Egyptian labourer. I felt our happy times were over. I was right. Only a month or so later we lost Jon Walley (relieved by a nice but nondescript doctor) and early in the New Year Mike Hennel went sick. I felt like a survivor myself.

During this time in dock we heard that the *Ark Royal* had been lost off Gibraltar. Now there were no carriers in the Mediterranean. At the beginning of the month Philip Vian (whom we had last seen on the blazing bridge of the *Afridi*), now a rear admiral, arrived as Flag Officer 15th Cruiser Squadron in the *Naiad*. One could be sure of fireworks with him.

Loss of *Barham*

So, with virtually no chance to shake down, we sailed from Alexandria on 24 November 1941 resplendent with new paint and a black top to our foremost funnel, indicating that we were now the Flotilla leader, 2nd D.F.

It was another 'club run' with eight destroyers escorting the *Queen Elizabeth*, flying ABC's flag, *Barham* and *Valiant*. The cruisers were well ahead, hoping to intercept an enemy convoy heading for Benghazi. We were in support in case the Italian heavy ships came out.

At about 1630 on the following day, I had just come off watch and was about to have a cup of tea in the wardroom when there was a heavy explosion. The alarm bells rang and I ran up to the director, to see the *Barham* listing well over. As usual when the bells went, one looked up in the sky for aircraft. But soon it was evident that this was no bombing attack. She leaned over very rapidly, lying for a moment on her beam-ends. Then with a tremendous explosion her magazine blew up. The moment was captured on film by a press reporter in the *Valiant*, who was next astern. One could hardly believe that anyone would survive. But *Hotspur* and others picked up several hundred, including Vice-Admiral Pridham-Wippell with whom we had been through so much. We remained on the screen and returned next day to Alexandria.

There were, of course, investigations and a board of enquiry. It appears that *U331* (Kapitän-Leutnant Hans-Dietrich

Freiherr von Tiesenhausen) had passed between *Jervis* and ourselves. An echo on *Jervis*'s asdic had been classified 'non-sub' due to its being a rather woolly wake echo, and the submarine itself was not contacted due to their relative speeds. Both destroyers and the U-boat were going quite fast at the time. As far as I know, *Griffin* never got a contact at all. There has been some controversy over the whole matter. But my feeling has been that by now none of our destroyers was fully efficient in the anti-submarine role, having been continuously employed on other sorts of work, and *U331*'s attack was executed with skill and daring.

Ironically, von Tiesenhausen now lives quite close to me in Canada, and is a good friend of mine. He has a tale to tell too. Decorated by Hitler with the Knight's Cross, he was sunk in late 1942 in the western Mediterranean by the British, and taken prisoner. Among others he was interrogated by my old Captain (D), George Creasy, then director of anti-submarine warfare. Von T was sent to Canada as a prisoner of war and not released until 1947 when, having lost everything in East Prussia, he came back to Canada and started again at the bottom. I have a sketch, which he made of the scene, viewed from his periscope. The news was hushed up for several weeks, an extraordinary thing considering the number of spies in Alexandria, including the Japanese consulate, which was still at large, though not for much longer.

Next day we went out again with *Naiad* and *Euryalus* along the coast. By this time, the latest British offensive in the desert was gaining momentum. Our sweep was to intercept enemy reinforcements, but, finding nothing, Vian decided to liven up proceedings by bombarding Derna airfield. This seemed rash to me as one could almost see the Ju.87s taking off in retaliation. And so they did, but this time they were not nearly so effective. We felt much happier with our Oerlikon guns, and none of them dived so low as in the past. I do not know whether, at last, the bravest of their pilots had been eliminated or whether they had gone to Russia; but for the first time in nearly a year we felt less defenceless.

Pearl Harbor

Now things started happening thick and fast, both on our level and in the world. On 7 December 1941 came the attack on Pearl Harbor, but we were too busy to think much about the ramifications of it. Next day, Tobruk was relieved. A few days later, we put in there. It was fascinating to see by day what had hitherto been dim black shapes. The devastation was every bit as bad as expected. A short run to the perimeter revealed horribly wrecked tanks, trucks, trenches, flies and a nasty smell. I was rather glad to be a sailor. Then we heard of the loss of *Prince of Wales* and *Repulse*. It seemed that none of the lessons we'd learned the hard way in Norway, Greece and Crete had been taken to heart. By now, one had somehow been inured to bad news.

On 13 December 1941, we were at sea again with Admiral Vian, this time to try to intercept an enemy convoy in the Ionian Sea. Once again, no luck, so back to Alexandria. A few miles outside the swept channel, in pitch darkness, we were keeping station at twenty knots. There was a flash and a heavy explosion. It was the cruiser *Galatea* hit by torpedoes from *U557*. These cruisers hadn't much protection and she sank quickly. We went to pick up survivors. It was the usual miserable business: oil everywhere, men shouting in the dark, bodies, some with and some without life. The wounded didn't last long; many of them were burnt. As usual, one couldn't remain stopped for long for fear of being picked off by the U-boat, which couldn't be far away. And there weren't enough destroyers to hunt her. Among those we rescued was a pressman called Larry Allen who did nothing but complain that he had been 'slapped on the deck like a wet fish'. There was nothing wrong with him, while there were many others who needed urgent attention. We had never had much opinion of what are now called the 'media', but this one was rock bottom.

Back in harbour that night we landed the 'Galateas', tried to clean up the oily mess and went off to sea again to meet the *Breconshire*, which was on her way back from Malta. By now, there were only ten operational destroyers in the fleet, so we were kept busy.

Queen Elizabeth and Valiant

Nothing much happened on this trip. We returned in darkness on the 18th. Next morning there was a surprising amount of activity around the battleship anchorage. It turned out that, as we were entering the boom defences the previous night, some Italian 'chariots', or one-man submarines, had entered with us and placed their limpet mines under the *Queen Elizabeth* and *Valiant*. The mines exploded later leaving the two battleships sitting gently on the bottom. Our battle fleet was now reduced to zero.

This was not the end of the bad news. Next day, Force K operating from Malta ran into a minefield off Tripoli. *Neptune* and *Kandahar* were lost – the former with Dick Coulton, our late sub and the famous Rory O'Connor, one of the outstanding captains in the Navy. In addition, *Aurora* and *Penelope* were damaged, so our Malta force was wiped out.

It was therefore a gloomy Christmas, which we spent in harbour. I drank a lot of rum going round the mess decks in the traditional style, followed by some lethal cocktails in the wardroom. For the second (and last) time in my life, I could rightly be described as too drunk to perform my duties. I retired to the heads whence I was rescued and put to bed by (was it?) Jon. When I came to, I was not pleased with myself, the ship, or the world.

Meanwhile the army had been moving forward in the desert, captured Benghazi on the 24th and were at the western end of their run – El Agheila – not long after. This meant that the desert airfields were again in our hands, so it should be much easier to supply Malta. January was spent in escorting ships either there or to supply the army along the Libyan coast. It was a pity that we had so few ships left, merchant or naval, to exploit the situation and stop the enemy doing likewise. Unfortunately this relatively easy state of affairs didn't last long. Rommel attacked and by the end of January, our army was reeling backwards again. This time they halted a little west of Tobruk so that although Alexandria remained quiet, the Malta runs were as bad as before – threatened from the desert and from Crete and with very little fighter protection. In addition, the German U-boats had been reinforced, not having apparently suffered much loss.

Malta Convoy

While these runs were unpleasant enough for us, it was hard to imagine how the crews of the merchant ships must have felt. They were the main targets, had little defence, and could do little to avoid the bombs. They were the heroes.

On 12 February, we set out again with a convoy for Malta. This time there were only three merchant ships. Next day was a heavy one, with attacks all day. In the evening the *Clan Chattan* was hit, some ammunition exploded in a huge ball of flame and she had to be sunk. Her sister, the *Clan Campbell*, was also hit and sent in to Tobruk. After we left, the remaining ship, the *Rowallan Castle*, having been turned over to escorts from Malta, in turn was hit and had to be sunk. So no ships at all got through, although some empty ships got out.

We were sent off to Haifa, where usually a couple of destroyers were stationed. Looking forward to another nice easy period, we were surprised to be recalled to Alexandria.

PART IV

The Far East and Back

Indian Ocean

On arrival we fuelled, took on stores and in company with *Decoy* were detached to join the Eastern Fleet in the Indian Ocean. At least we had got out of the eastern Mediterranean with a whole ship – the outlook there was not promising. But perhaps it was even less so in eastern waters where the Japanese already had a reputation. Previously underestimated, now I think they were overestimated to some extent. The cry went round: 'they never miss', and had to be proved wrong.

One loss by this move was Mike Hennell. He had been in hospital in Alexandria with measles or mumps and we sailed without him. A few months earlier, on one of our evenings ashore in the Monseigneur, we had dared him to pick up an exceptionally lovely young lady who was under the eagle eye of an apparently rather forbidding mother. Mike succeeded in charming both the girl and her mother and eventually even her father who for a long time was kept in ignorance of the liaison. Mireille – for so she was named – saw a lot of Mike when he was sick. They were married in Alexandria and have been admirably suited ever since. After the war, she was a perfect tri-lingual wife for a British naval attaché in – of all places – Rome. Mike once told me that after they had been married, no less a person than King Farouk took an interest in Mireille, sending flowers and other attentions. She remains the only girl of my acquaintance who has turned down a king.

But we digress. Once again, down the Red Sea to Aden. This time we passed on to Bombay. By now the fiasco at Singapore and the Java Sea was nearly over. By some chance, as we sailed through the Arabian Sea, we received the last signals of the *Exeter* as she was trapped and sunk by the Japanese near Java. One wondered what we were getting into. But we had been lucky once again. The Mediterranean destroyers detached earlier had both been sunk and their crew made prisoners of the Japanese.

Bombay was quite another world from Alexandria. The nearest Japanese were several thousand miles away, yet from the general feeling of panic, you felt they were just around the corner. My thoughts went back to the barmaids in Dover, cheerful and cool. We spent about ten days here during which time I managed to get the entire hull and upperworks chipped of old paint and repainted by a huge throng of spindly-legged Indians. A refrigerator came on board, ostensibly for the sick bay but somehow ended up in Nick's cabin.

We went ashore to the Willingdon Club and the Taj Mahal Hotel, but found the local people not very nice or even friendly. The captain's secretary, Jenkins, found himself accused of being 'just a chicken: you don't know what it is to be menaced by a wounded tiger'; and so forth. One wasn't surprised by the fall of Singapore.

A pleasing contrast was the attitude of the USS *Boise*, which had come to Bombay for repairs, having run on an uncharted reef during the invasion of the Philippines. 'Just give us a dock, and if the locals can't do it in short order, we'll do it ourselves.' I wonder how they'd have got along with the Trade Unions in a British yard. *Boise* was a lovely ship, clean, well designed, with lots of anti-aircraft armament and fifteen 6" guns. Why couldn't we have that?

Eastern Fleet

We left Bombay without regret, steaming south to join the newly constituted Eastern Fleet. We joined it off Ceylon.

It then consisted of the *Warspite*, repaired in the USA after Crete, wearing the flag of our old chief, Admiral Sir James Somerville. Another dirty job for him but encouraging for us as we had great confidence in him. There were no less than three aircraft carriers: *Formidable* (repaired after Crete damage), *Indomitable* (brand new, having missed the Singapore disaster due to running aground in Jamaica while working up), and the small and ancient *Hermes*. Unfortunately, the number of aircraft available for these ships was very small. There were a few ratty old cruisers, but two large ones, *Dorsetshire* and *Cornwall*. And about sixteen destroyers, nearly all, like ourselves, getting worn out and in constant need of repair. A few days later we were joined by four 'R' class battleships, unmodernized from the First World War – virtually floating coffins dragged in from convoy escort duty. While to the eye this was an impressive array of naval might, in practice we were desperately weak in everything that mattered. We hadn't had a chance to train together, exercise or work up to any sort of efficiency as a fleet.

And by early April all the indications were that the Japanese striking force that had pulverized Pearl Harbor was about to enter the Indian Ocean. We fuelled quickly in Colombo and put to sea again so as not to be caught in harbour. We cruised about to the southward, daily expecting news of the Japanese Fleet. It was unpleasantly hot, especially down below where scuttles and hatches were closed for action. But the sea was a glorious deep blue, the sky, sometimes clear and sometimes full of enormous columns of cumulus, below which there were deluges of torrential rain. Passing through these, we stripped and had most refreshing shower baths, but soon dressed again, covering the skin as far as possible. I had seen enough of burns not to be caught in shorts.

Up to 5 April there were still no signs of the enemy; I can't say I was sorry. Now we know that Admiral Somerville realised that our only hope was to stay out of range during the day – a difficult task in view of their enormous strength in carrier aircraft – and close at night, hoping to inflict as much damage as possible. But we couldn't afford another disaster as there were no ships to replace losses at that time.

Addu Atoll

So we steamed southwest to the secret base, Addu Atoll in the Maldive Islands, where there were some oil tankers and supply ships. I found the approach fascinating, through fairly narrow gaps in the coral reefs, clearly visible in the brilliant water. The usual white sandy beaches and scrubby palm trees looked to us at the time very unparadisial. At anchor, it was exceedingly hot. We were short of water. You couldn't swim because of the sharks or go ashore because we were at half an hour's notice. We were told that they weren't missing anything because there was malaria and elephantiasis and the coral gave you sores (I believe that nowadays people pay to go there). There was no mail.

About this time, I got prickly heat and a 'desert sore' on my knee, which wouldn't heal and was itchy and unsightly. I was exceedingly tired. We didn't stay long. At 0700 on 5 April 1942 at last news came of the Japs. They were (at their closest) 150 miles away, comfortable distance for an air strike. And they had five of the six large aircraft carriers which had attacked Pearl Harbor. Our Admiral hastened to sea with his faster ships, leaving us to follow with the four old 'R' class battleships. For the next three days, we manoeuvred about between Addu and Ceylon with the rather forlorn hope of delivering a night attack, and with the fervent prayer that we would not be spotted by day.

We were lucky. The Japanese were ignorant of the Addu base and looked for us in Colombo and Trincomalee. Not far away they found the *Dorsetshire* and *Cornwall* and sank them expeditiously. Soon after, they found the *Hermes*, without aircraft and, sadly indeed, sank not only her but her escort, the *Vampire*, and the small destroyer *Tenedos*, which had miraculously survived Singapore and the Java Sea. The wretched Catalina flying boats, which tried to shadow, were shot down. However, the defences were ready for the massive air assault they made on Colombo, and a squadron of Fleet Air Arm Hurricanes gave them the first bloody nose of their career. Another of my term, Paul Pierano, was shot down and killed in this engagement.

In the next few days, another Japanese force was busy in the Bay of Bengal, far away from us. We intercepted signals from merchant vessels reporting air attack, sinking and so forth. Nothing could be done. As our fuel began to run short, our fleet returned to Addu by another channel – Veimandu. A day later, we started the long retirement to Kilindini on the coast of Africa.

I remember how thoroughly fed up we all felt at this undignified retreat, mingled with relief at not participating in what might have been a spectacular defeat. We had Admiral Somerville to thank for our survival with some honour. I do not think the nation, or Mr. Churchill, realised what we owed him. But one does not get recognition for avoiding defeat. I, for one, felt embittered at the pacifists who had led us into this situation, which we had seen coming for so long.

Mombasa

The Japanese Fleet vanished eastwards as suddenly as they had come. A month or so later they met their own nemesis at Midway. The long passage to Mombasa was depressing. Apart from being very tired, I had recently been suffering from toothache, my own fault entirely because it had been some time since I had bothered to brush my teeth properly. After, say, a middle watch followed by dawn action stations at five thirty, a day's work and a first watch from eight to midnight, I just fell into my bunk at the earliest possible moment. The toothache got worse so I was thankful to find there was a depot ship in Kilindini with a dental officer. In true naval style, he whipped out one tooth and did some carpentry on some others. It was a great relief to be free of pain and the threat of air attack, all at once. Apart from the odd submarine, the enemy was now many hundreds of miles away.

But the general heat, discomfort, lack of mail and the moral effects of 'running away' took its toll among some of our scallywags from the Alexandria detention quarters. Some of them refused duty one afternoon, leading to some unpleasantness after which they found themselves back in DQs, this time in Nairobi, which is probably what they wanted anyway. It was a most unhappy time. One of my few pleasures was hearing Admiral Somerville standing on the torpedo tubes of an Australian destroyer, lying alongside, telling their sailors what he thought of their attempt to set fire to a nunnery in Mombasa, under the impression that it was a house of another sort. I wish I could remember his exact words.

Madagascar

Early in May, we were off to Madagascar. At least this was an offensive move, although only, once again, against our late allies. The operation was entirely successful and the useful base of Diego Suarez was taken, to deny it to Japanese and German submarines. It was none too soon, for the old *Ramillies* was actually torpedoed by a two-man submersible carried by one of the big Japanese boats. Our part in the operation was not exciting as it consisted of screening the carriers. Then it was back to Kilindini. Here there was good news, for me at any rate. The *Duncan* arrived, a properly fitted flotilla leader, and as she had more accommodation and better communications, an exchange was made. Nick and his dismal staff went there and we got her CO, Lieutenant Commander 'Hooky' Rowell, with whom I got along very well.

Malta Convoy Again

No sooner had this change been effected than we were off again – back to the Mediterranean. So, round the Horn of

Africa, hot and windy, rather rough. A sailor from one of the other ships fell overboard and was taken by a shark. Up the Red Sea and back through the canal to dear old Alexandria. The occasion of our temporary transfer was, of course, another Malta convoy. Things were getting rather desperate there now; so one was to be run from each end of the Mediterranean. But our end was not to get an aircraft carrier because they had to face the Japanese in the Indian Ocean.

We left on 11 June 1942 – Operation Vigorous with Admiral Vian in charge in the *Cleopatra*, the *Naiad* having recently been sunk. This time we had a substantial escort – seven cruisers and twenty-six destroyers – but no heavy ships except for the quaint old *Centurion*. This old battleship, built in 1910, had for years been used as a radio-controlled target ship in peacetime. She was full of concrete, and it was hoped that bombs would bounce off her. She was not very convincingly disguised to look like a 'King George V' class battleship from the air with a view to discouraging the Italian fleet a bit. But her passage through the canal had been greeted by ribald remarks from soldiers on the banks, as her canvas and plywood gun turrets flapped in the wind. Still, she'd take some of the heat off the merchant ships – and us.

In the event, the operation took five days and was unsuccessful. Gradually we lost the merchant ships to bombing, which was intense, though we did get some fighter cover. On one attack there were seventy Ju.88s, so a great deal of ammunition was expended. Clouds of dust went up from the *Centurion* who steamed blithely on. But eventually, when right in 'bomb alley' off Benghazi, ammunition began to run short and the Italian fleet put to sea. The C-in-C (now Admiral Harwood) recalled us so the operation was abandoned.

That night there was an attack by E-boats, which sank the *Hasty* (who had survived so much) and put a hole the size of a small bus in the cruiser *Newcastle*. Next day was more rewarding, and with our nice new Oerlikon guns we shot down a Savoia torpedo bomber and thought we had a Junkers. The wretched *Airedale*, escorting a damaged merchant ship to Tobruk (still in our hands, but about to be lost), was set upon by thirty Junkers and sunk. On the last night the cruiser *Hermione* was sunk by a U-boat. So it was back to Alexandria again with rather a bloody nose. The Gibraltar convoy had just as tough a time but succeeded in passing two ships to Malta. We got none.

It was while this was going on that Rommel was making his triumphant way along the desert to El Alamein. All hell broke loose in Alexandria, where papers were burnt and evacuation prepared. Fortunately, for our peace of mind, we were spared this, being given time only to fuel and return to the Eastern Fleet, escorting the damaged *Newcastle*.

Operation Vigorous has been well described by A.E. Pugsley in his book *Destroyer Man*. He was captain of the *Paladin*, also on the screen.

Strangely enough, this moment, although I didn't know it, marked for me a sort of turn of the tide. Until this time, almost all the aircraft we had sighted were hostile. From now on, it was to be the reverse. Years later, I obtained a photograph of *Griffin* proceeding at high speed away from the camera. Johnny L-B was asked why we were 'running away'. He replied, 'We were always running away.' From now on, on the whole, we did the chasing.

The trip down the Red Sea and southwards along the coast of Somaliland was agonizingly slow. Socotra on the port side seemed to lurk there forever. The monsoon was blowing freshly, the seas heavy against us and the wounded *Newcastle* was labouring, sometimes reduced to 2 or 3 knots. I don't think she was in any danger, but we were worried about her. However, we got her down to Kilindini at last. It seemed to be a long way from the real war.

Mayotte

The next operation was almost comic. Although Madagascar had been occupied in May, there remained the Comoro Islands, still in French hands and situated at the north end of the Mozambique Channel through which a large volume of merchant shipping passed coming up from the Cape. Our task, which required one destroyer, was to take over the island of Mayotte and lay moorings there for Catalina flying boats to patrol the channel. It was not expected that there would be any resistance, but one could not be sure.

So we sailed southeast from Mombasa and, true to form, appeared off Mayotte at dawn. The initial problem was to find the way in because the island was circled by coral reefs. The rather ancient chart showed the entrance channel, which one could negotiate safely by keeping two baobab trees in line. The difficulty was to locate the right trees, as there seemed to be a lot of them. However, the reef could be seen clearly from the masthead and we had a good star fix as dawn broke, so we found the place.

After gingerly edging through the channel, we worked up to full speed in the inner lagoon to steam round to the main settlement Dzaudzi and anchorage. I was still boarding and landing officer, so on the way in I got my party of braves armed in the usual somewhat amateur-looking fashion of landing parties – white 'flannels', shorts, black boots, green webbing belts and gaiters, carrying unwieldy rifles and bayonets. I had my .45 revolver, and as soon as we had anchored, off we all went ashore in a couple of boats; about thirty of us, not knowing quite what to expect.

There was no one about at all. After a while a very black, very sleepy Negro appeared and, surprisingly (though it should not have been) addressed me in excellent French. He much admired, he said, the 'vitesse' with which we had entered harbour. It turned out, as might have been expected, the Governor was 'up island' with a lady friend. There were no armed forces. It was the easiest conquest I ever made.

In proper revolutionary tradition, we took over the post office and telephone exchange (in which Alexander Graham Bell would have felt quite at home). These buildings were decorated with faded, peeling portraits of Marshal Pétain, and the slogans of Vichy – honneur, patrie, etc. No one seemed to care. Then I went back on board for breakfast, bearing croissants. We spent a happy few days in this fascinating place, laying the moorings. They had been lifted on board by crane at Mombasa, but were much too heavy for our davits. So we had to fall back on good old seamanship (rightly defined as an obsolete method of lifting heavy weights). Apart from one of the big concrete blocks running away rather rapidly, all went well. I wonder if they are still there. We also did a little target practice with our after 4.7″ guns which had recently been remounted. We succeeded in blowing to pieces my only cabin trunk, which had been brought up out of the tiller flat in a fit of clearing up. There wasn't much to do ashore because we remained at short notice for sea. A number of sailors got very drunk on local brandy; we embarked a little lemur with a striped tail to add to our livestock, and a chameleon for the wardroom flies. In fact, this island produces a lot of civet, which, when combined with the flowers of Grasse in Provence, makes superb scent.

Nairobi

When this idyllic interlude came to an end, it was back to Kilindini where further good news awaited. We were due for a boiler clean, and went alongside the depot ship for ten days – things were less hectic than in the Mediterranean. While alongside, an invitation came from Nairobi to send a party of sailors up for a break. Oddly enough, all the officers felt too tired to go, so I volunteered and didn't regret it.

After being cooped up in a hot steel ship for months, this was like a fairy tale. The trip up and back was superb: comfortable bunk, good food, and memorable views of Kilimanjaro and big game. On arrival we were 'taken in hand' and offered so many choices that it was hard to decide. It would have been a waste to lie sleeping so it was car trips, parties, girls, swimming and so forth. Altogether a wonderful break. I returned to the pea-soupy heat of Mombasa refreshed in body and mind. Even my 'desert sore' started to get better and was soon healed.

Zanzibar

Life on our return was quite peaceful. The old 'R' class battleships had been dispersed back to escorting important convoys, being too ancient and unmodernized to join the fleet proper. We were employed on patrols, escort and exercises; the only danger was from the very few submarines which might come so far from German bases in France or the Japanese base in Singapore. Only one rather slapstick exercise remains in my memory. We were to exercise the local defence troops on the island of Zanzibar. We approached, naturally, at dawn, and a romantic hour it was too. Tropic seas, palm trees, white sandy beach and a smell of cloves.

I, being the boarding and landing officer, came ashore with my braves. We landed unopposed and were thinking how un-alert the defenders were when down from the trees descended a company of black troops in khaki shorts and little tarbushes, grinning very wide grins. These were not funny grins but fearsome ones, and for a while we thought they were going to be nasty. I didn't like to start anything, so allowed them to pop us in the local jail for a while until the umpire ended the exercise and we returned on board with mutual expressions of esteem. I feel I'm the only person in town who has been in jail in Zanzibar.

Over, then, to Dar-es-Salaam, presumably to reassure the locals. We spent a couple of nights here, finding it, too, a fascinating place; clean and orderly, even now reflecting its brief German occupation before the First World War. In the harbour mouth were still the rusty remains of the dock, which the Germans had used to block the entrance in 1915. On our way back to Mombasa we looked in briefly at Tanga, and that was then the end of our East African tour. When we got back, we received orders to return to England.

Passage Home

By now we were not fit enough mechanically or, indeed, humanly, to be much use against the Japanese; so we were delighted to hear the news. We sailed in September 1942 and had to go by the Cape route because the Mediterranean was now virtually closed.

The trip home was interesting and on the whole uneventful. A wonderful night in Durban, where we were met by the celebrated 'lady in white' on the dockside and exposed to more hospitality. Then a few days in Simonstown. I took the train to Cape Town and fell in love with that unhappy country where my father had been during the Boer War. In Cape Town, we embarked a load of gold bullion, each ingot the size of a brick in a wooden box. Its arrival on board was heralded by an armada of motorcycle police, flashing lights, an armoured car and guards armed to the teeth. When we later unloaded the stuff in England, a quiet gentleman in a grey suit took delivery and drove away in a plain van. Then ploughing westward through heavy seas, and turning north, we proceeded up the west coast of Africa.

Pointe Noire, near the mouth of the Congo: wine and French bread. Lagos, hot and dirty. Freetown, where we went alongside the *Dunluce* (or was it the *Edinburgh Castle*) to find her full of rats; ashore for a bathe at Lumley Beach and to marvel at the variations in the human frame exhibited by the topless ladies en route. Bathurst, a collection of shacks (or so it seemed) at the mouth of the Gambia River.

Ever since leaving Simonstown we were receiving the Admiralty reports of U-boat dispositions. By now, they were quite thick on our route so we had to zigzag and be alert. We were much intrigued at the apparent accuracy of the positions given. Only in recent years has the work of the O.I.C. [Admiralty Operational Intelligence Centre] been revealed. In fact, at this time we had temporarily lost the ability to read the German cyphers, so much of the reports was based on intelligent guesswork. It was in this area that some months before the *Laconia* had been sunk by a U-boat with much loss of life, including the brilliant Leo Tillie, who was on his way home having been relieved as sub of the *Hotspur*.

It happened that as we were going north, the Operation Torch convoys for the invasion of North Africa were going south. We never knew of their existence. In any case, the number of U-boats caused us to be detached for a while to escort the old battleship *Royal Sovereign*, which was on the way to the USA for a refit. We headed for Bermuda with her, being shadowed by two U-boats, which could not overtake us. It was decided that, if they remained in touch for another day, we would have to stay with her all the way. To my disappointment, they did not and we turned back when a little short of Bermuda. George Clayton Greene, who was in a destroyer, which did go on, met his fate in Philadelphia, married her, and is now a US citizen. Such are the chances which seem to govern us.

We merely refuelled in Punta Delgarda (port wine with the friendly Portuguese), then on the last lap, put in to Moville off Londonderry for fuel having met and escorted the *Nea Hellas*, a large liner. The green of Ireland almost hurt the eyes but the eggs and fresh vegetables were welcome. It was the end of October and thus strangely was fulfilled a prophecy made to Johnny Blackmore at the pyramids in Egypt about sixteen months before, when he asked a seer, when, if ever, we should get home. A gentle trip down the Irish Sea, broken by a fruitless search for a downed airman, brought us to Southampton, to the very dock from which I had sailed to join *Griffin* very nearly four years earlier. I was the only member of her peacetime crew still serving in her.

Dockyard officials swarmed on board. Half the crew went off on leave and we started to run down. We were de-ratted – a process in which the ship is sealed and abandoned to some lethal gas for forty-eight hours. On opening up, a cat strolled out. I was a trifle concerned because now all the stores missing though enemy action, neglect or misappropriation, and unaccounted for, would be found to be on my charge.

Hooky Rowell left very soon, so I remained for the day of reckoning.

I needn't have worried. A Canadian commander, H.F. Pullen, arrived on board one day to say that *Griffin* was to be converted to an escort destroyer, taken over by the Royal Canadian Navy and renamed *Ottawa*. Pullen tried very hard to retain the name *Griffin* (which had in fact been held by a predecessor on the Great Lakes in 1912, I believe). But he was overruled by the politicos. He told me that the Canadians were not in the least interested in the stores lost or otherwise, and would start again from scratch.

He only wanted a history of the ship's wartime activities. Over some gin, I gave it to him. So HMS *Griffin* (H31) became HSMCS *Ottawa II*, which retained the pennant number. The original HMCS *Ottawa* had been sunk in 1942. Since then the successive holders of the name, *III* and *IV* have kept the connection with the old name in many ways. There is an HMCS *Ottawa* (H31) Association which publishes a newsletter called the *Griffin*. Those who have served in these ships are known as Griffins, and when *Ottawa IV* sailed for the Gulf War in 2002, she flew at the yardarm the White Ensign of the old H31.

The old ship survived the war, having sunk three U-boats. She was eventually stripped down and employed as a fast transport to repatriate service men who didn't mind discomfort to get home early. She ran seven or eight shuttles across the Atlantic taking three and a half days at twenty-five knots. Pretty good after nearly ten years of hard running. She was eventually broken up at Sydney, Nova Scotia. I wonder who has her bell.

By some chance, her brass and wooden nameplate from the afterscreen above the wardroom is now hanging on the wall of the Naval Museum in Esquimalt, BC.

Leaving *Griffin*

I was sad to leave the *Griffin* after nearly four years. She had been a lucky ship and, excepting for one short period, a happy one. But she was now outdated and I was keen to go on to a modern ship. I spent a week or two in Southampton turning the ship over to the Canadians, and re-establishing contact with my future bride-to-be who was by now a naval VAD [Voluntary Aid Detachment] at Haslar and seemed to be having a good time, one way or the other.

I took an interminable train journey to West Kirby, Cheshire to stay with my parents. I had to stay the night in Liverpool as the last local train had left. There was an officer's club, which provided beds and synthetic breakfast. After a tasteless meal of powdered eggs, I returned to my room to find that someone had stolen my baggage. This was a poor start to a rather disappointing leave. England was cold and dismal. The only bright lights in that area were in Liverpool, and that city was bombed and blacked out. However, there were people and parties. The large naval element was concerned with Atlantic convoy work and their experiences were not really in line. I did not feel much like discussing mine with my parents and this, I fear, disappointed them. My father, by now 68 or so and past retirement, still struggled in to Liverpool to examine recruits. He was tired and grey.

In due course I visited the Admiralty to enquire about my future. The Naval Assistant to the Second Sea Lord, (NA2SL), the arbiter of our destinies, was Commander St. John Tyrwhitt, son of the well-known admiral. I had met him when he was captain of the *Juno* in the Mediterranean before she was sunk off Crete. He asked me whether I wanted to 'specialize'. This was a major decision, vital to the direction in which one's future career would go. I knew that some of my contemporaries had been 'railroaded' into various specialist courses. I said that I didn't see any point in going ashore to do courses in the middle of the only major war I was likely to see, and that I'd like to stay in destroyers, please. He was very pleasant and said that, in that case, I could be the first lieutenant of the *Savage*, a new destroyer now building on the Tyne. She was to carry a new experimental anti-aircraft armament and was thus rather a plum. I was delighted, and spent the rest of my leave in a much better frame of mind.

PART V

The Tide Turns

Savage

The captain was to be Commander Cosmo Gordon, an old destroyer man. I corresponded with him and we both seemed happy. A few days later I heard from Johnny Lee-Barber, now to be captain of the *Opportune*, asking me whether I'd like to come as his first lieutenant. This was a real dilemma. I admired Johnny and would have loved to go to sea with him again. But I had already warmed to my new ship and didn't feel I could just tell Cosmo Gordon that I'd changed my mind. I must admit that I also fancied building a brand new ship with all the opportunities to get things done my own way from the very start.

So in February 1943, just after my 25th birthday, I set off for Newcastle where the *Savage* was building at Hawthorn Leslie's yard. I found some rather gruesome 'digs' in the city but soon moved into a small hotel, which was quite agreeable, although on civilian rations I felt hungry all the time. I even found myself eating the odd rock-hard bun left over from the other inhabitants' teas. But there was plenty of beer, very friendly natives and plays and concerts to go to with them.

One of the tricks of a pleasant life was to get to know some 'transport' Wrens. I had never come across Wrens before and was tremendously impressed by their efficiency and cheerfulness. They often managed to be in the right place at the right time with their cars. I usually caught a morning ferry across the Tyne, having waited on a windy pontoon downwind from a glue factory. It reminded me of Alexandria. It was good, though cold, to see an English spring again.

After a month or so, Cosmo arrived and I started to get to know him. He was a large red-haired Scot with big bushy eyebrows. He rarely spoke. We lunched together on his first day and I was wondering whether he was human, when he stared across the tables for a long time at a young family and announced at last, 'That little girl isn't going to drink her soup.' It was a while later when Dick Birks (a lone Canadian among us Brits) went into Cosmo's cabin to get him to sign the correspondence. Cosmo was in the armchair, reading *The Times*. 'Go away. I'm busy,' he said without looking up. He was true to type.

I thoroughly enjoyed the three months standing by the ship as she was completed. It was a great rest physically, and fascinating to watch her take shape, growing from a mass of rusty metal into a form with a life of her own. Hawthorn Leslie's were a good firm and very helpful. Just before the war, they had built the *Kelly*, which became Mountbatten's ship. They had put in all kinds of special items for his lordship. When I tried to get some of them for us, the reply was, if you care to telephone the King, perhaps he'll use his influence for you. However, they did us very well considering it was wartime.

One thing had repercussions. To prepare us for service in the Arctic, the entire inside of the living quarters was sprayed with asbestos for insulation purposes. It was exactly forty years later that I showed ill effects from this, resulting in a lung operation, which I trust has solved the problem. The dour but efficient Scots-Canadian surgeon ended my final examination with the cryptic words, 'There's nothing more I can do for you.'

When the tripod mast was stepped, I had my half-crown placed at the foot of it in the Roman tradition, looking to the omens for another lucky ship. It worked. Gradually the officers and key members of the crew assembled. A good lot, though we never got to know each other as well as the 'Griffins'. The chief, another fine old Scottish ex-warrant officer, was 'Livy' Livingstone. Taylor, the navigator, Dick

Birks the lone Canadian – he must have found us a strange lot to begin with. Many years later I talked to him at Montreal. I had just come to Canada. He was going to live in England. Then McGillivray and Miller, two very efficient RNVR sub-lieutenants.

I had a couple of lovely warm weekends in the country before commissioning day arrived on 24 May 1943. From then on, trials of every kind, and down the river to sea. Although we didn't know it, the tide of war had turned while we were building. Until then, our side had been fighting a rearguard action at sea and ashore. From now on, we were winning and one felt the difference, especially with regard to the air. Hitherto we had seen very few friendly aircraft; from now on, we hardly saw any enemy. It was ironical that in *Savage*, we now had the ability to shoot them down. On 10 June, we sailed for Scapa Flow to join the Home Fleet.

Home Fleet

Scapa Flow has often been described, and I for one was far from delighted that it was to be our base. The Home Fleet heavy ships lay in the Flow while the destroyers, which were at last appearing from the shipyards in fairly large numbers, were moored at buoys in Gutter Sound. For many days in the year, it was too rough to get ashore. When you got there, you found little but a bleak moor, some windswept sheep and a few nissen huts, which provided a cinema and a beer bar. There was also a squash court where I played a couple of times, but found myself so unfit that I was more likely to perish there than at the hands of the Germans. The weather was usually cold and windy, but just occasionally in summer there were some perfectly lovely calm days in which the daylight lasted almost round the clock. In winter, the constant gales and darkness led one to drink when not asleep. Nor was there any sense of history – those hairy Vikings never meant much to me although one had to admire their seamanship in these stormy waters. Some of us were bird-watchers (RN Bird

Watching Society, motto: one good tern deserves another).
Girls were of course non-existent. Altogether it was a dismal
change from Alexandria, though we spent so little time in
harbour that it didn't matter all that much.

We had about a month to work up, with all the usual gunnery
torpedo and anti-submarine exercises. Our experimental 4.5"
gun worked well and could elevate to nearly 90 degrees –
perfect for engaging Ju.87s. As it turned out, we never saw
one again. The torpedo practices were less successful.
Simon Warrender, son of Lord Bruntisfield, Civil Lord of
the Admiralty, was torpedo control officer, a quiet, serious
old Etonian. At first, he never seemed to get it right. On the
occasion of our 'passing out' firing, we were to fire all eight
torpedoes at a live target. We advanced at speed, the sights
came on, triggers were pressed, and – nothing happened.
Cosmo, an old hand, merely signalled, 'That was a dummy
run,' and went round again. The error was righted but we still
wondered how we'd do in action. In the event, we needn't
have worried.

Political Interlude

At last, we were pronounced fit for war, and the ship felt good
and efficient. Our first task was an unusual one. We were
detailed to take the First Lord of the Admiralty (a civilian of
course), A.V. Alexander and the Minister of Labour, Ernest
Bevin, from the Fleet Flagship to a remote Scottish loch –
Loch Eriboll – for a short holiday.

It was, as usual, blowing hard as we left the Flow, and
the Pentland Firth was unpleasant as we plunged into a
heavy head sea. Ernest Bevin started off quite cheerfully and
interrogated the Chief Yeoman of Signals on the bridge about
the nature of his job. Having heard his replies, the Minister of
Labour (on whose mind the manpower situation must have
been weighing) went so far as to suggest that such a job could
be done by a woman. He must have lost several votes there
and then. He then retired to the captain's cabin. Alexander

stayed up a bit longer. A 'Barracuda' torpedo bomber flew by – known already to one and all as one of the worst designs anyone could be asked to fly. 'I was largely responsible for that fine aircraft,' intoned the First Lord. Silence indicated that we all thought as much. He then required a signal to be made to a small convoy, passing by. 'Greetings from your First Lord.' The Chief Yeoman could hardly conceal his pleasure when he reported, 'No reply, sir.'

To get to my cabin from the bridge in rough weather I had perforce to go through the captain's day cabin. This strange arrangement was due to our experimental gun turret. On my way down, I knocked and was admitted, to find Ernie Bevin stretched out in an armchair looking rather green. 'Here lad,' he said, 'Have you ever seen anything like this?' He then lifted his shirt, lowered his trousers somewhat and revealed a mass of scars and stitch marks. I made some appropriate remark and passed along, wondering a bit about our leaders. To give him his due, I later developed an admiration for this man. I cannot say the same of A.V. Alexander.

Gibraltar and Faroes

Immediately on return to Scapa, we refuelled and sailed for Greenock and thence Gibraltar, for what purpose I cannot remember – it was probably to escort one of the big ships on her way to the Mediterranean. A quick turn round found us back in Scapa four days later for yet more exercises and screening of the big ships. Among these was the USS *Alabama*, a large new battleship, which we took to sea one day with our own *Duke of York* to shoot at an aircraft-towed target. The *Duke of York* fired everything she had, but the target sailed blithely on, apparently undamaged. Then the *Alabama* let fly in an eruption of yellow smoke and flame from all over the ship. The target disintegrated instantly and that was the end of the exercise. There must have been a message there for our distinguished gunnery officers.

Boiler clean time came round soon after, which meant a quick trip to Rosyth – at least somewhere near civilization. Forty-eight hours leave to each watch didn't allow anyone to go far. I spent the time in Edinburgh quite agreeably.

The next couple of weeks were spent operating from Skaale Fjord in the Faroe Islands, another rather dismal part of the world even farther north than the Shetlands. It rained and blew hard all the time – it was now late September – and we were at sea every day. I did get ashore once and went for a long walk on moss-covered hills, running waterfalls everywhere, lonely sheep and seabirds and occasional little shacks with sod-covered roofs. Hardly a human being was to be seen.

One of the operations concerned the USS *Ranger*, an aircraft carrier, but the weather was too bad for flying and we all returned to Scapa, arriving early in the morning of 7 October.

That afternoon we were off again, this time to Gibraltar in the company of three new American destroyers, the *Capps*, *Hobson* and *Forrest*. It was heartening to have our allies in company. After those lean days in the Mediterranean and Indian Ocean, we seemed to have large numbers of powerful ships, and to spend a great deal of time at sea. But somehow it is hard now to see just what we were accomplishing.

Our American friends amused us a lot. On arrival in Gibraltar on a flat calm, sunny day, we went alongside one of the moles. The *Capps* tried to come alongside us. She made a mess of it twice, and the third time came a bit closer, very slowly, close enough for one of their heaving lines to bridge the gap. One of our sailors grasped our end, whereupon the man on the *Capps* dropped his. A bullhorn from her bridge cried plaintively, 'Jesus Christ, forecastle, what do you think you're doing?' Their discipline seemed to be different from ours. The reply became a catchword around the *Savage* for many a day.

We were to have one night in Gibraltar. Our sailors were intrigued when three Americans started over their side to paint from 'break to break'. They were men under punishment. Our chaps commiserated with them for losing their evening ashore. 'Don't worry,' they replied, 'we'll have this done by six and see you in the Metropole.' They did, too, with their excellent paint and huge brushes. It would have taken our chaps all day.

It was on this run that I made (or failed to make) a quick decision that has stayed in my mind. We were steaming at over twenty knots on a dark night. The radar was not performing well and it was hard to keep in station at the distance we were keeping from the guide. I was quite tired, as we'd had many days at sea. A lookout reported a light on the starboard beam and I looked for it myself without seeing anything. He insisted that it had been there – just a quick flash. To turn towards and investigate would have meant losing the 'fleet', making appropriate signals and, if there was nothing there, spending a long time trying to catch up and find our guide again. I decided to ignore this report and continue our course. I have sometimes wondered whether it might have been some wretched airman ditched in a dinghy. But perhaps it was only a star.

North Russia

We were back in Scapa on 18 October, having been at sea for twenty-six days, broken only by less than a day at Gibraltar. We had five days in and out of Scapa with anti-submarine exercises in the Flow, and the embarkation of a lot of special stores for a destination as yet unknown. Obviously something interesting was up, so our spirits, which had been dulled by the recent monotony, rose somewhat.

On the 23rd we sailed, to arrive at Skaale Fjord once again. After refuelling, we were off at midnight on a quick passage to North Russia. This was new ground to me, and exciting. Only a few days earlier the midget submarines from Scapa had succeeded in immobilizing the *Tirpitz* in Northern Norway, so it seemed likely that convoys would start again now that the days were getting short.

The passage to Kola Inlet only took three days at twenty-six knots. This was easy. The weather was kind; overcast and grey as usual but quite calm. There was no sign of the enemy. Kola Inlet proved to be a dreary place, black and white, and shades of grey. The dark rocky shores were uninviting as were the inhabitants. A Russian pilot came on board at the mouth of the inlet to see us through the minefields and strings of black buoys supporting the anti-submarine nets. Otherwise, he proved to be useless, and later in the evening he got drunk and passed out. In an attempt to lift him onto a couch someone touched his pistol, which momentarily brought him to life. He was aware enough not to be parted from that. After oiling from a decrepit Russian tanker, we shifted berth early in the morning to Polyarnoe, the naval base.

This I found quite fascinating. Our Russian 'allies' were there in some force, particularly their long black submarines. Their destroyers looked rather Italian in style and as we found later, did not venture very far out. But they liked to come in with us, having done the last 100 miles or so, when the worst part was long over.

It appeared that the reason for our comfortable berth in the naval base was that the Russians wanted to look at our new experimental gun turret. Otherwise, we usually found ourselves out in Vaenga Bay, away from the Soviet ships. Anyhow, it was not long before the British Naval Officer in charge of our mission asked us to have a party of Russians on board to look around, stressing that no technical information was to be given – just a quick look around. So we had a group of five or six of them; fairly young, intelligent and not so thick-looking as most of the others we saw. They spoke good English and chatted amiably though humourlessly in the wardroom over a gin before the tour. On being told that we could not divulge any technical information, they nodded agreeably but then proceeded to pump anybody they could buttonhole on the way round. We didn't like their attitude much. In return, we were not asked on board any of their ships, but instead had a late evening at the Red Navy Club where we sat through a performance of song and dance given by the Northern fleet choir. They were most professional, though one wondered how they had time to practice, unless they spent most of their time in harbour – which proved to be the case. The club was festooned with red and gold banners, the inevitable huge pictures of Marx, Engels, and Lenin and Stalin, the 'gruesome twosome'.

There were also some relics of the Allied occupation in 1919 – a comparatively recent occurrence, which must have impressed them deeply and could account for at least some of their suspicion and hostility. One never had a chance to tell them that none of us would really want that piece of real estate. Sentries were everywhere and it was hard to get anywhere near the town. What one did see was not prepossessing. There were many Mongolian types unloading stores in a desultory way, watched by yet more armed sentries. A lot of very square women wielded shovels and kept the paths clear of snow. There was a smell of drains.

All in all, not a savoury place and one had little desire to return. But we were to be back. Although our sailors were rather pro-Russian on arrival, having been fed with 'good old Uncle Joe' propaganda, it didn't take long to change their views generally to ones of scorn and disgust at our reception. We spent four days in Polyarnoe, during which time I attempted, for the first time, to ski. Equipment was available from the naval liaison people and we all went off a mile or so to a place called (by us) Death Valley. There wasn't much daylight and there were lots of bumps and rocks. We were of course put to shame by little Russian boys on what looked like barrel staves rushing down the slopes with broad grins and great élan. They seemed to be the only agreeable people there.

On 2 November, it was off to Vaenga Bay to top up with fuel, and we left that evening to meet convoy RA 54, empty ships returning to the UK. It was an eight-day trip in dull miserable weather, cold and dark. But the enemy didn't bother us. We passed close to Bear Island – 74.30 north – the furthest North I'd been so far.

Boiler Clean

Having delivered the convoy safely to Seidisfiord in Iceland we set off for Scapa and Rosyth for a boiler clean. There was good reason to be thankful that boilers needed periodical cleaning; otherwise, it seemed that we would never get any leave. From Rosyth one could reach civilization, though with only forty-eight hours for each watch it was no good trying to go far. Unfortunately, there were now facilities at Scapa Flow for cleaning boilers alongside the depot ship. From there, there was nowhere to go at all. On this occasion at Rosyth, I had a terrifying experience. I found myself the only man at an all-ladies dinner – a guest of my cousin Helen at the Fleet Air Arm base at Donibristle, where the Wrens had a mess. It was a good dinner but I had to 'say a few words' after it. After our six-day break, it was back up to Scapa and another twenty-one days at sea.

Murmansk Convoys

This time it was another convoy for Murmansk – JW 54B. Once again the trip was uneventful, though cold, rough and tedious. Our arrival in Kola Inlet was eerie. It was 2 December and pretty dark. There were great swirls of fog, black water, and white snow-covered ice. The bare rocks on either side of the inlet were menacing and only constant sounding of mournful foghorns of various pitches broke the silence. Altogether, it was a forbidding place. I felt that if Hell were to be cold, this would be a foretaste of it.

After fuelling, we actually got a night of rest, leaving next afternoon on a direct passage to Scapa. The seas were, as they say, mountainous. I don't think I've ever seen it rougher, windier, darker and colder. We plunged into it, keeping it on the bow. All passage along the decks was stopped.

The ship shuddered violently and rolled horribly. This was a test of the excellent seagoing qualities of our destroyers, though one felt we were near the limit.

Sadly, a young sailor called Gregory was washed overboard and vanished without trace. He must have fallen or been swept from the after radar position – well above deck level – he being a radar operator. It was hopeless to try to find him, though we searched for a while. In the state of the sea and the temperature of the water, he had no chance of survival. We arrived at Scapa five days later, much battered and saddened by the loss of such a young man – he was only 19.

A New Captain

For some time now, Cosmo Gordon had been unwell. He had been at sea in command for many months and was, I suppose, in his mid-thirties – getting a bit old for this kind of battering. A relief had been asked for and duly arrived on board the day after we reached Scapa. I was sorry to lose Cosmo. I think we had got along very well and I respected his outward imperturbability. We were to meet again in 1948 when he was on the staff in Malta, and responsible for the living conditions of the men of the fleet. I had command of the *Rowena* but was in the Red Sea, leaving my wife to find somewhere to live in that bombed-out island. Accompanied by a newborn son, she found a shooting lodge a long way from anywhere, with no doors or windows or electricity. Cosmo came to inspect it. He might well have pronounced it unsuitable, although there was not much alternative. However, he stretched a point and let her stay. But he did remove the live ammunition from a little pistol, which a well-meaning Maltese police inspector (Freddie Bencini) had given Faith to keep under her pillow.

To return to our narrative, Michael Meyrick, son of my first captain at Dartmouth, relieved Cosmo. Michael was a kind man, but I always found him rather nervous and serious, perhaps over-strained. With all our time at sea I never got to know him personally very well. But he was good enough to trust me to get on with running the ship my way.

Our day in Scapa was largely occupied (for me) by a board of enquiry into the loss of A.B. Gregory. This was held on board the Canadian destroyer *Haida*, recently arrived (she is now lovingly preserved at Toronto). I believe that no fault was found with our arrangements and Gregory's loss was considered unavoidable under the circumstances.

The Sinking of *Scharnhorst*

Off we went again to Kola Inlet, this time in the august company of the commander-in-chief, Admiral Sir Bruce Fraser, flying his flag in the battleship *Duke of York*. The weather had moderated by now so this trip only took four days. We had a battleship with us, it was too dark for aircraft, and we were going too fast for effective U-boat attacks, so it was a nice cosy passage. We had a day in Vaenga Bay. The admiral hobnobbed with the Russians, even charming some of them. I don't know whether he told them that he had been a prisoner of the Bolsheviks in the Caucasus back in 1919. Meanwhile I went skiing again, followed by a get-together with our flotilla mates, of whom we had so far seen little.

Next day, 18 December, to sea again with *Duke of York*, the cruiser *Jamaica* and three others of our flotilla, *Scorpion*, *Saumarez* and the Norwegian *Stord*. The latter must have been feeling groggy because they had fuelled from a Norwegian oil tanker and the resultant mutual drowning of sorrows had led to some delay in the fuelling programme. One thing that still puzzles me is how the Norwegians, with identical ships, managed to keep theirs spotlessly clean whatever the weather. They just didn't seem to get dirty – whereas ours. . . !

Evidently, something was in the wind because all the way to Iceland we were engaged in a rather strenuous series of exercises, including a 'night encounter', which we didn't welcome at the time as it cut into our short ration of sleep, but which later proved its value. Once again, an easy high speed trip to Akureyri. Our little group of six ships anchored in that rather dreary harbour. My evening was made by an invitation to dinner with Admiral Fraser in the flagship. He asked the captains, executive and engineer officers of the group so the three of us, Michael Meyrick, Livy Livingstone, and I put on our bow ties and were very soon overwhelmed by the charm of the Great Man.

After dinner he told us what was up. He had good reason to believe that the German battle cruiser *Scharnhorst* would attack the next convoy. At the time, of course, we assumed that this intelligence must have come from Norwegian sources. Now we know about 'Ultra'. The C-in-C ran over his plan, which was to keep in the offing until the convoy was attacked and then get between the *Scharnhorst* and her base. He demonstrated his tactics in the time-honoured way with pepper pots and so forth, and said that he planned for *Duke of York* to open fire at 12,000 yards while we destroyers went in to attack with torpedoes. He was so simple, cheerful, and amiable that I felt it was rather like an exercise. And indeed we rehearsed the action next day, with *Jamaica* taking the part of the enemy. The whole thing felt good.

We left Akureyri at 2030 on 23 December 1943 under strict radio silence, steaming well to the southwest of the convoy which was already well on its way. For the next two days, we plunged north-eastwards as the weather deteriorated. By Christmas day, there was a full gale from the southwest and it became difficult to keep the ship on a steady course. Movement along the upper deck became a matter of clutching onto the lifelines and watching your chance. I don't remember much of Christmas dinner other than hanging on to the table as the plates vanished when the ship surged with the swell.

It was, at this time of year, dark until well into the forenoon, and the dim light faded early so that station-keeping was an exhausting business of peering through wet binoculars for hours on end, aided by radar reports via a telephone (our surface radar set was far from the bridge in those days, and there was no nice green dial to look into). We were in two watches – four hours on and four off – so that by the time you got down below and thawed out it seemed nearly time to struggle into your outer garments again.

It was during the morning of the 26th – Boxing Day – that signals from the convoy escort told us that *Scharnhorst* was indeed out and had been intercepted by our cruisers. The day's action is well known. Admiral Burnett skilfully parried each of the enemy's thrusts until in the afternoon it became clear that he was running south and heading for home. It seemed almost too good to be true that we were in a position to intercept, and our presence might be unknown to the enemy. But so we were, and I well remember the mixed feeling of elation and apprehension when *Duke of York* made radar contact, and the star shells of the cruisers burst forth and fell on the far side of the *Scharnhorst*. We moved ahead to clear the range and went to action stations.

Gunnery Duel

My station was on X gun deck, aft and well away from the bridge in a position to take over command if the party on the bridge and the captain were wiped out. It was a good vantage point, slightly exposed, I felt, but it was good to have a cheerful, heavily muffled gun's crew around to chat to. It wasn't long – about 1650 – that *Duke of York* (and *Jamaica*) opened fire at 12,000 yards, just as Bruce Fraser had planned. Then, for about an hour, we were witnesses to a spectacular duel in an extraordinary setting of darkness, wind, and heavy seas. Both ships were firing shells fitted with tracer, so that one could follow their leisurely flight, ending in a forest of splashes around the targets. The guns thundered, the wind howled, and great flashes marked the salvoes. All in all, a splendid sight, especially as they weren't firing at us.

Torpedo Attack

After a while, the range seemed to be increasing and we were ordered in to attack with torpedoes – the be-all and end-all of the destroyer man. We managed to work up to some thirty-four knots with the heavy swell on the quarter. It was hard to keep one's footing, and we hung on to guns and ammunition lockers for life. Orders from the bridge came to illuminate the enemy with star shell, so off we popped with X gun, using flashless cordite. After a while, the *Scharnhorst* must have seen us, as they started to shoot with their secondary armament 5.5" guns, but they also seemed to be firing bursts above us. At one moment a young sailor on my gun (I forget his name) fell to the deck, then got up again, then snatched off his tin hat with a yell. A piece of shrapnel had penetrated his tin hat, knocked him down, and then taken a moment to burn through the woolly layers of his balaclava helmet. He later had a great tale to tell with his shell splinter. I too still have one which fell nearby. He was our only near-casualty on X gun, but a few men were wounded up forward, including the coxswain who was able to continue to steer – an arduous business in that sea.

It was an exhilarating half-hour, though a little frightening, as it seemed we would never catch up. In fact, we were lucky because *Scharnhorst* had suffered several hits, which impaired her gunnery efficiency, and there seems to have been some disagreement on board about which of several targets should be engaged. At one stage, the words 'do you expect me to fire at shadows?' are said to have been used.

To our astonishment, just as we were feeling that we'd never get up into a good firing position, the battle cruiser turned about and came down out of a cloud of smoke, placing us in a perfect position on her bow. It turned out that *Scorpion* and *Stord* had been hitherto unobserved and had worked their way up *Scharnhorst*'s other side. She had turned to avoid their torpedoes and was about to run into ours.

She was a superb sight, massive yet elegant. She appeared to me to be a light grey colour in the light of the starshell, which were falling eerily about her. On our bridge, Simon Warrender had to alter his sights very rapidly and to have the tubes trained on the opposite beam. This time, he got it right. We got off all eight torpedoes at very close range – about 3,000 yards. It seemed very close indeed.

Astern of us, *Saumarez* went even closer and rather unwisely (to my mind) opened fire with her 4.5" guns, which could have done little good against such an opponent. This attracted a salvo or two from *Scharnhorst* which killed or wounded about twenty men and resulted in *Saumarez* being able to fire only 4 out of her 8 torpedoes. It was an exciting five minutes.

As soon as we had got rid of our 'fish' we hauled away into the darkness. We claimed three hits – justifiably, I think. I certainly saw one large explosion, which might have been from more than one torpedo. At all events, our job was done and within minutes we were drinking hot cocoa and blessing our lucky ship. None killed and only a few wounded, and not badly at that. Could it have been my coin under the foremast?

As we lay off, keeping an eye on the wounded *Saumarez*, the rest of the fleet moved in and started to pound the wretched *Scharnhorst* to pieces. All we could see was a heavy curtain of smoke lit up by huge flashes as the *Duke of York* closed in. Soon she was so close that her shells, flying almost horizontally, failed to penetrate the target's deck armour, but they must have made a dreadful shambles of the poor victim. Eventually almost every ship with any remaining torpedoes closed in and fired them at the now helpless and hapless ship. As always, one had to admire their bravery.

In all the smoke and spray, there seems to have been some doubt as to the moment of her sinking, and several rather anxious signals came from the flagship seeking confirmation of the fact. *Scorpion* picked up a mere thirty survivors and *Matchless* another six, all that remained of more than 2,000 men. Most of us felt sad but mighty relieved that it was not ourselves floating about in the smoke, debris and oil, heaving in the heavy swell and icy water.

When all was over, *Scorpion* and we escorted *Saumarez* towards Kola Inlet, slowly at first but gradually increasing speed as she got matters under control. The weather moderated and we had an uneventful passage, arriving off Vaenga Bay at 2000 the following day, the 27th, in pitch dark, as usual. There wasn't much rest, however, as fuelling was slow. We anchored at last in the middle of the night. Next day we were off again to Scapa, arriving four days later.

Duke of York led the way in, followed by *Jamaica* and the destroyers. We were irritated by *Musketeer* whose division hoisted strings of flags indicating how many torpedo hits they claimed. Seeing that by the time they arrived on the scene, *Scharnhorst* was stopped and none of her guns were firing, we felt that this particular method of showing off was in poor taste in our company. All we got was six days alongside the depot ship *Tyne*, boiler cleaning and replenishing ammunition and torpedoes. I was hauled off to give a talk on the radio, but I have no idea what I said until I saw some extracts quoted in a book, years later.

On 2 January we celebrated a belated Christmas, but Scapa is no place for entertainment, and there was some resentment when *Musketeer* and her gang went down to Rosyth for their boiler cleans. However, c'est la guerre; our turn would come. Michael Meyrick told me that he was doing the honours and awards and was recommending me for a bar to my DSC as he had been such a short time in the ship before the action and had found everything working like clockwork. However, we settled on the 'chief' as I already had one, and Livy had done wonders down in the engine room. I eventually got a 'mention'. I've sometimes since regretted my uncharacteristic generosity. Later there was also a Russian medal up for grabs, and we drew lots for it among the crew. I'd have liked one of these because you got a small sum annually in roubles and free travel on the trams in Archangel, along with pregnant women.

Ironically, it was forty-five years later that, along with a lot of other Canadian and British veterans of this campaign, I did get a Soviet commemorative medal as a part of a general thawing of relations. Our own people never gave any specific recognition of this rather arduous and at times dangerous duty.

On the subject of medals, when we dined with Sir Bruce Fraser, he showed us the proposed ribbons for the first campaign medals of the Second World War. He had been asked for comments. I noticed that the first one was to be called the 1943–? Star, and wondered why there was to be no recognition of those who had served since the beginning in 1939. (In WWI they had a 'Mons Star' for 1914). In the event, the qualifications became even less demanding, the medal became known as the 1939-45 Star, available to almost everyone who served at all and therefore nearly valueless. It became known as the 'Spam' medal, dished out like that horrid form of ration. He also showed us the Africa Star, which was to have a special rosette for those who served there at and after the battle of El Alamein at the end of 1942. From the naval point of view, this period was one of far less danger than the months before, when there was no fighter protection. So the rosette was sometimes called the 'Umbrella'. Both medals and those which followed were rather cheap and nasty in all aspects.

More Russian Convoys

Wherever they took place, one was always thankful for boiler cleans which allowed a few nights of uninterrupted sleep, even though one tended to stay up late anyhow visiting friends in other ships. Luckily, nobody had yet invented a boiler which did not need cleaning, as there were always more tasks than ships. Our five day rest over, we spent a couple of days doing anti-submarine and anti-aircraft practices and then sailed for Loch Ewe where we picked up some merchant ships for the next Russian convoy (JW 56A) and escorted them to Seidisfiord in Iceland.

The weather started wildly enough, but as we reached the 'shelter' of Seidisfiord a full gale blew up. Like so many Icelandic fiords, this was a forbidding place, steep and deep with black snow-capped mountains on each side. These provided a nice funnel for the icy winds. After a few hours at anchor, we started to drag our anchors uncomfortably, so at one in the morning, pitch dark and snowing horizontally, we had to feel our way out to sea for safety if not for comfort. Next day we were able to come in again and get alongside a tanker for fuel, but left before dawn for Akureyri where we spent another night.

On 27 January we were off at last to join convoy JW 56A bound for Kola Inlet. This time there was little or no danger from surface ships, and not much from the air. The U-boats were the main enemy apart from the weather which was mostly foul. The U-boats had by now developed a nasty kind of torpedo which followed your propeller noise and, if successful, tended to blow off your stern. The riposte was to tow a bundle of metal rods which jangled together and attracted the homing torpedo to a spot well astern. Of course, one had to be careful when recovering the tow that there wasn't a torpedo on the end, following like a faithful bloodhound. In addition, on sighting or detecting a U-boat, we had to perform a side-step method of approach, or to slow down to reduce noise. All these precautions tended to limit our anti-submarine effectiveness. To add to these problems, the water layers – warmer Gulf Stream flows over cold arctic waters – made detection difficult and sometimes nearly impossible. On the way this time, we carried some civilian scientists who required us to stop every now and then to lower a bathythermograph on the end of a long wire to take readings. Being fleet destroyers, we had less anti-submarine practice than our Atlantic counterparts. However, escorts were now much more numerous and the occasional small aircraft carrier was beginning to appear, so that surfaced U-boats could be caught before they got close. And in really rough weather they could not operate at all.

I believe that some ten U-boats concentrated against JW 56A. We had nine destroyers and two corvettes led by the new flotilla leader *Hardy*, commanded by Captain Geoffrey Robson, another old hand from the Mediterranean and a most distinguished destroyer captain. All went quietly for the first four days; the weather had settled down and we had no difficulty in refuelling from the tanker *Noreg*, using the astern method in which one had to grapple a line from which eventually one could haul in a floating hose towed by the tanker.

At about 1600 on 25 January, the U-boat attacks started. Anti-submarine conditions were poor, and we were reduced to dropping depth charges at random to try to put them off their stroke. But three merchant ships were hit, one of which, the *Penelope Barker*, we were detailed to help. She sank very rapidly and all we could do was to find what survivors there might be in the pitch dark, cold black water. We soon found a group of them, some on a raft and others floating. As usual, it was an uncomfortable business stopping while there were so many U-boats about. By now, we had a pretty good rescue organisation set up – especially the rope nets dropped over the side, up which a survivor could climb if he had enough strength. If not, we had to go down the net and help him up. There was one such group of three men, two of them trying to support a black man who was clad only in a singlet and trousers. I was over the net with a splendid young Yorkshire sailor called Nunwick – strong as a horse and trying to lift the black man out of the water. He was cold and oily and kept slipping back. Eventually, Nunwick and I fell in with him; our hands had got cold and slippery and we lost our grip on the net. At this moment, the ship drifted away and we were left on our own for what seemed a long and lonely time. I was worried that perhaps a U-boat alarm might cause the captain to get quickly out of it. Luckily, this didn't happen and it was just a matter of manoeuvring to get us back. It may have been only five minutes or so, but it was quite enough, as the cold water had begun to seep in. Luckily, we were by now, superbly equipped (compare 1939!) – kapok overall suit, woolly hat, inflated lifebelt, battery driven red light, whistle and a looped rope around the body for easy recovery. But it was a *mauvais quart d'heure*, the only time I had to swim in the whole war, which was just as well because I am a poor swimmer. Nunwick and I got back on board, had a stiff whisky, and didn't even catch a cold. The wretched negro had fallen back in the water when we lost our grip of him and we never saw him again. The other survivors were a most agreeable lot of Americans who were, naturally, most grateful for their rescue. Months later, a parcel arrived from the USA. It turned out to be a gramophone record which they had made, sending thanks and good luck messages by each individual – a nice American touch which was much appreciated.

There seem to have been a lot of torpedoes around that night, but the only other casualty was the *Obdurate* who managed to make port later. On the 27th, as we were nearing Kola, out came four Russian destroyers; too late, as usual, to be of any use, but in time to look as though they had been part of the escort. That evening we arrived in Vaenga Bay and had a pretty good night in. Early next morning, alongside the *Noreg* to fuel, then alongside the jetty to disembark survivors and stores. That evening, off to sea again to meet the second half of the convoy, JW 54B, which followed a few days behind and was about to run into a U-boat line. Next day at 2200 we joined the escort, bringing the total of destroyers and corvettes to about twenty, a formidable force. But even so we had another sticky night, full of attacks and counter-attacks. At four in the morning, *Hardy* was hit aft by an acoustic torpedo and had to be sunk by *Venus*. Several others had near misses, but as far as I know *Savage* was not attacked.

Polyarnoe Again

We were getting rather tired, all the same. We were back in Vaenga Bay on the 31st at 2000, fuelling from our old friend

Noreg again. Next morning early, it was up again to shift berth to Polyarnoe. This time, for once, the Russians were almost friendly and we were bidden to another entertainment at the Red Navy Club. Jon Walley (now in the *Milne*) and I went, suitably fortified with cherry brandy. After the choir performance there was music and a dance floor around which sat some rather square-shaped women, some of who danced with Russian officers. Naturally, we approached the 'girls' to ask for a dance. The lady would look quite horrified and glance across to one of the commissar officers, who would give a little nod, and the unfortunate girl, terrified, would do a quick round of the floor and retreat rapidly to her bench again. The feeling of fear was palpable, and once again, one wondered about a system like that. Next day, Jon and I went skiing again in Death Valley and wandered about the dreary streets, full of sentries and large women sweepers. There didn't seem to be much damage from air raids, though Murmansk itself had suffered severely.

It was on this occasion that some officers in the *Milne* let it be known that the Russians had arranged an elk hunt for us. Participants were to meet on the jetty at 1000. Quite a large group turned up, suitably attired for this form of sport. There were several relatively senior officers who, having hung around waiting for half an hour, discovered that the whole thing was a hoax. They were displeased.

One more night's rest and we were off to escort RA 56 – a group of thirty-seven ships, mostly empty, on the way home. We had a large escort, some twenty-three ships; a sign of the more affluent later years in the war. I believe that on this occasion the German air force reported our convoy quite early on, but gave an easterly course, thereby joining the reciprocal club. Thus, we had an uneventful passage and lost no ships. But the other enemy, the weather, was always with us and I remember so well being unable to stay in my bunk for fear of being pitched out, and trying to 'nap' on the deck. The other trouble was cold feet (both kinds?). While one could keep one's body reasonably warm, even on an open bridge, I found it impossible to keep my feet warm in spite of fur-lined leather boots. So working watch and watch, one would get off the bridge, say, a little after midnight with four hours off before the morning watch. The first hour of the four would give little sleep, as I can't sleep until my feet are warm. But by putting an electric light bulb in each boot, I could at least start off warm for the nest watch. I got used to the resultant atmosphere. Of course, one had to be called about twenty minutes before appearing on watch, so that one could pull on all the warm clothing again and clamber up the swaying ladders. Once or twice, I remember sitting on my bunk and just cursing; then being deposited on the deck again as the ship gave another lurch. Better, perhaps, to be an engineer, but still I would rather be on the bridge when things are happening.

One such moment occurred when we were chasing a contact on the north side of the convoy. I was in my bunk when the alarm bells went and was just getting to the door when there was an almighty shudder and a roaring noise. I was up the ladder like a startled monkey. By the time I got to the bridge, we realized what had happened. The 'contact' was ice, and we had run full tilt at twenty knots into the edge of the ice pack south of Bear Island. Damage was not actually great (unlike the *Titanic*, we hit head on), though we wrote off our asdic dome and had some leaks in the lower compartments. The bright side was, of course, the need for a docking on return home. And after five or six days at sea we were detached to Scapa whence we went on to Hull for repairs – the first glimpse of civilization for what seemed an age.

A week in Hull allowed three days leave for each watch. I remember telephoning Faith, admitting I had grown a beard, and weakly removing it at her behest. It was my Mark II, and a great asset in the frozen wastes of the Barents Sea. But not really tenable in London.

Out again on 17 February, to arrive at Scapa Flow to 'celebrate' my 26th birthday. I remember being alongside the Canadian destroyer *Algonquin*, and our wardroom going over after dinner to make a call, all being dressed as clergymen with our collars reversed; only to find ourselves upstaged by the wardroom of the *Mahratta* who were already there, sitting cross-legged on the deck, dressed as Arabs. That ship had quite a reputation, being known as the 'Mad Hatter', but sadly had only a few more days afloat. The captain of *Algonquin* was Debbie Piers, whom I got to know much better years later in Kingston, Ontario, when he was commodore at RMC. After he retired, he was for a while the Agent-General in London for Nova Scotia. A splendid fellow who had a good ship.

Last Russian Convoys

We left again on the evening of 20 February for Skaale Fjord where we picked up the next Russian convoy – JW 57. It had been decided to run one large convoy this time instead of two smaller ones, so we had a strong escort of seventeen destroyers and, praise be!, a small aircraft carrier, the *Chaser*. This made a great difference to our lives and kept the shadowers away and the U-boats down. This was just as well as there were some fourteen of them after us, and we were spotted on the second day out – earlier than usual. There ensued a week of alarms and excursions by night. Conditions were vile as always, but we were able to keep a double screen going, spending a lot of time chasing echoes and dropping charges. Our sole loss was the poor *Mahratta* which was hit by a homing torpedo and sank quickly with the loss of nearly all hands. But this time we lost no merchant ships at all and at least two U-boats were sunk.

So we arrived in Kola Inlet on the 28th – for the last time, as it turned out.[12] After a couple of days in Vaenga Bay, it was off again with the returning convoy – RA 57. Lots more activity of the usual kind, starting with thick fog and snowstorms. The *Empire Tourist* was hit and sunk in the convoy by one skilful attack and many torpedoes were about, of various nasty kinds, pattern running, and homing. *Milne* and *Swift* were just missed, but three U-boats were sunk mainly by *Chaser* aircraft. This time we felt we really had the upper hand at last. The next convoy – JW 58 – arrived unscathed having sunk four U-boats. But that was after our time. Change was in the wind.

South Again

Hardly had we got back to Scapa on 9 March 1944 when we started on a series of exercises – low and high angle gunnery shoots and bombardment practices. With the 'second front' expected this summer, this looked interesting. Tarbat Ness and Culbin Sands were the targets, and we embarked some soldiers – bombardment liaison officers, or BLOs – a new breed to us, for the practices. A few odd jobs screening carriers and escorting *Warspite* to Rosyth, and the great news arrived that we were to refit at Immingham.

This would be none too soon as I, for one, was getting very tired. In the last six months, we had been at sea for 143 out of 180 days, and not very comfortably at that. I was feeling the strain quite a bit and at one stage, when we got back to Scapa after the *Scharnhorst* action, found it hard to talk to anyone I didn't know. This soon passed off, but a rest was indicated. Anyhow, we arrived at Immingham on 2 March and had exactly a month in dock – a wonderful break. By late April the days would be longer and the weather (with any luck) a bit better.

I rang up Faith who was at Westcliff, near Southend, looking after sailors, as a VAD. We met at the Savoy Hotel and had a lovely evening. I managed to cover a fair amount of ground, between staying with my parents in Cheshire, my aged uncle in Beaconsfield and partying in Liverpool and London. I even got on horseback a couple of times. One unusual event was a lunch at the Savage Club in London, given in our honour to celebrate the *Scharnhorst* action. The club's members are distinguished literary or thespian figures and the thought of an after-lunch speech in such company would have spoiled the meal had not our hosts been so delightful and easy. My main recollection is chatting to Tommy Handley (ITMA – *It's That Man Again*) who was every bit as amusing as he was on the best radio show of the war. I spent that night, for some reason, at Hampton Court Palace, staying with the Kennedys, she being the widow of Captain Kennedy who was lost in the *Rawalpindi* early in the war. She had a lovely 'grace and favour' residence in the palace.

Back on board, there were the usual businesses associated with a refit and much dirt and noise of hammering and riveting. We emerged in good shape with fresh camouflage paint, all white and shades of light green and blue – thanks to Peter Scott who was the first to persuade Their Lordships that dark colours showed up more at night than light ones, especially in northern climates.

Back to Scapa

After a few days of trials, we were back in Scapa on 24 April. As usual, there was a full gale blowing so we had to anchor for a few hours before struggling into the destroyer moorings in Gutter Sound. The next two weeks were fully occupied with practices, especially anti-aircraft, anti-E-boat, and bombardment. It was pretty obvious that D-Day for the landings in France was approaching and that we would be there. Anything better than Scapa and Kola.

On 3 May we left with two carriers, *Fencer* and *Searcher*, for an air attack on Kristiansund. After a postponement due to weather, some 18 Barracudas and 20 Wildcats flew off and attacked German convoys with some success. On the 12th we were off again with the battleship *Anson* and the carriers *Furious* and *Victorious* to have another shot at the *Tirpitz*, which had been quite badly damaged by a similar attack in April.

At this stage, the Fleet Air Arm aircraft could not carry big enough bombs to sink this huge ship, but at least she could be kept out of action. Unfortunately, the weather closed in again so the operation had to be cancelled. So it was back to Scapa on the 18th and another week of practices. But our time there was coming to an end.

Prelude to Overlord

On 26 May, with much joy we sailed for Sheerness in the mouth of the Medway and Thames estuary. Not that Sheerness is much of a place either, but it is close to civilisation and the English Channel was more inviting than the Barents Sea. It was during our few days stay in Sheerness that the secret orders for Overlord – the Normandy Invasion – arrived on board. As second-in-command, I got to study them and was tremendously impressed. Every detail had been thought of, every movement dovetailed in. I had until now been quite ignorant of the Mulberry harbour projects, the pipelines, the jetties and ramps, the breakwater of sunken ships – all the details which are now history. What a contrast to our hand-to-mouth experiences in all those evacuations! By now, our air superiority was unquestioned and I started to have confidence in the result. Until now, I think most of us were a little apprehensive of the assault and feared another fiasco.

On 31 May, we went south for a patrol in the Straits of Dover, anchoring in Pevensey Bay. We were affording protection to some of the Mulberry ships and equipment and also, I believe, acting as part of the build-up of a feint landing in the Pas-de-Calais. Again, I felt, what a contrast to my experiences almost exactly four years earlier in these very straits.

We were back in Sheerness on 2 June and now only awaited the date of the expedition. I made a telephone call to Faith at Westcliff and had to be careful and discreet. Then a good game of squash, though hardly in condition for it.

Normandy Invasion

At last, on Sunday, 4 June 1944, we were off. But the weather was foul and the whole show had to be postponed twenty-four hours. When we finally left on Monday evening the weather was still foul, and we felt very sorry for the soldiers in their landing craft as they bucketed up and down. One school of hard-liners felt that seasickness would make them fight like tigers so as not to have to get back in the boats. But the weather did moderate as we passed through the Straits of Dover, escorting our group of tank landing ships.

Some way south of the Isle of Wight and north of the Normandy coast there was a sort of Piccadilly Circus where many groups converged before setting off to the coast and the landings. It being full moon, though cloudy, we could see a huge concentration of shipping on all sides, each carefully timed and in its right place. I couldn't sleep, other than the odd catnap when we were at action stations. Very early in the morning there was a roar of aircraft overhead as the airborne assault went over in their gliders. Our task seemed safe and easy compared to theirs.

At dawn, we were off the coast but to our disappointment we were not called upon to bombard – after all that practice. Perhaps they were preserving our experimental gun. We merely patrolled the eastern edge of the landing area to protect that huge mass of shipping against surface attack, which might be expected, from torpedo boats or E-boats from the direction of Le Havre. The first very brave attacks came when we were escorting one of the LST convoys and were away from the beach area. During it our sister ship the Norwegian *Svenner* was sunk by torpedoes from a force of German torpedo boats who could only have been a pin-prick against our enormous armada which I see listed as 7 battleships, 23 cruisers, 105 destroyers and many other types. The balance had changed with a vengeance.

In fact the whole operation from our point of view was, after the initial approach, a huge anti-climax. One had been expecting mayhem but it hadn't come our way. We never saw a hostile aircraft and nobody shot at us. The main worry was the pressure mines, which were at that time unsweepable, and caused us to go very slowly in shallow waters. As in

1939, my knees were slightly bent much of the time. But as soon as the landings got a good foothold, we were moved out to patrol on the eastern edges and further out to sea where the water was deeper. The only likely enemy seemed to be E-boats and U-boats, and we could well cope with those. So the next few days were employed thus with occasional alarms and excursions at night and some visits to Portsmouth or Newhaven for fuel, fresh provisions or mail. This kind of warfare in nice summer weather was almost agreeable.

The main incident of interest happened on 15 June. We were patrolling more or less on the meridian of Greenwich when a lookout reported an aircraft on fire, approaching from the French coast. This was followed by another and yet another. This seemed strange, and when Michael Meyrick arrived on the bridge, he remembered an intelligence report in which the first flying bombs were to be expected. These were, indeed, the V1s, or buzz bombs, and pilotless. Thus, I suppose, we saw the inauguration of the missile age, a historic occasion. There wasn't much we could do about them, except shoot at those within range. We heard from other ships that if you hit one it could go out of control and perhaps head for you – so we rather cravenly reserved our fire for those that had passed.

PART VI

The Final Victory

Temporary Command

On 17 June we were back in Chatham for a week's boiler clean. There could hardly have been a better place. We had a 'Chatham' crew and London was within easy reach. I went off to Southend to see Faith, went to the ballet with her in London, and took her to the Cavendish Hotel where we drank champagne with the redoubtable Rosa Lewis – a living piece of history if there ever was one. When I got back on board, I found that Sub-Lieutenant Miller, our sterling gunnery control officer, had been invalided with tuberculosis, the result I feel sure of those Russian winters. And, more importantly from my point of view, Michael Meyrick went sick indefinitely, leaving me in command.

I knew that there were many 'spare commanding officers' who had been stored up in reserve in case of heavy casualties during the landings. Every one of them was vastly senior to me and would undoubtedly be itching to drive a nice new destroyer like the *Savage*. However, the next day I was sent for by the C-in-C – no less a person than Admiral of the Fleet Sir John Tovey. He asked me a few questions about my experience and was quite charming. I was very conscious of the tremendous responsibilities that he had as C-in-C Home Fleet, Bismarck, Russian Convoys and all, and of his distinguished past as a destroyer captain himself, especially his brave efforts at the battle of Jutland. Eventually he asked me whether I felt I could take the ship. Answer, obvious. I left the Presence with the distinct feeling that he would be glad to swap places. With a final 'don't run aground going down the Medway', I was dismissed and returned on board as happy as I have ever been.

Next morning I took her down the Medway (with due care) to Sheerness and thence to an anti-submarine patrol off Beachy Head – exactly where we had patrolled four years earlier in harder times. As it turned out, I only had a little over a month in command, but it was fun while it lasted. We had a good crew, an agreeable wardroom and no problems. Most of the time was spent at sea in the eastern part of the English Channel, with occasional visits to Newhaven for mail, Spithead for fuel and replenishment, and sometimes two nights rest at anchor in Pevensey Bay.

Unfortunately, there was nothing dramatic to make a name with, and the E-boats kept their distance. We were, I suppose, mainly looking for U-boats because those that were fitted with 'snorkels' could and did operate in the Channel. On one occasion in foggy weather, I thought I had one for sure. The radar gave an echo about the right size, proceeding on a steady north-easterly course. We pounded off after it, taking the approved side steps against homing torpedoes. Then we sighted it, a grey object like a conning tower. It was an errant barrage balloon, floating along on the surface. End of excitement.

On another occasion, also in fog, we again got an interesting radar report; this time two echoes close together moving slowly towards Boulogne, then still in German hands. We crept up, got closer and closer, and still it cruised on. Then a lookout reported something high up in the air, looming out of the fog. It turned out to be a large crane. Some distance ahead of it was a very small tug, flying an American flag. It took a while before they answered our hails, and longer still before they would believe that they were headed for an enemy-held port.

The other members of our patrol were our old friends *Opportune* (Johnny Lee-Barber), *Obedient* (John Hodges) and *Orwell*. All were good to work with, and I saw quite a number of other old friends on our evenings in – Hugh Wilson in

Harrier, Phil May and Duncan Lock. I also caught a glimpse of the old *Griffin* again, now the *Ottawa* but looking much the same. She had just sunk a U-boat not far away. On one occasion, I at last managed to call on our 'real' Captain (D), Peter Cazalet in the *Saumarez*. He gave me the sad news that one of the dreaded spare COs would soon take over from me, but that I was assured of my own command as soon as possible.

So my days went pleasantly with good warm weather, short nights and agreeable company. I spent most of my time on the bridge, day and night, especially in fog of which there was a fair amount. This was now much easier on the nerves than in the old days before radar and 'Gee' navigation systems. In fact, I have always rather enjoyed being at sea in foggy weather with its whispers and eerie sounds, but equally have hated rough seas because I never really got over a nasty tendency to seasickness.

Well, at last my new captain arrived on 24 July. He was Wickham Malins, a much-decorated lieutenant commander whom I liked at once. He was most sympathetic and said I'd have my own ship in a couple of months. He wasn't far out. Very shortly after his arrival, we were anchored off Newhaven and I managed to get ashore to have a look at the 'plot' in the headquarters – a place that to some extent controlled the shipping in the area, and put us onto any enemies who might appear. This time there was, among the excellent Wrens who manned the plot, one with an exceptionally large stern. When her tea break came around, she jumped up, stumbled and knocked the table, whereupon most of the 'shipping' slid a mile or two westwards and had to be replaced as far as possible. This didn't do much for our faith in the plot. Sure enough, that evening there was an E-boat alarm – I think they damaged the Canadian *Rimouski* and sank two small merchant ships off Dungeness. We went off in chase. But after some long-range gunnery they got away, having easily the legs of us, and vanished into Boulogne. After this, we had a few days at Spithead, one of which was occupied with some anti-aircraft practice using the new VT (variable time) fuses in the shells. This admirable device (invented in Britain) had been obtained from the Americans – from my point of view, four years too late. It was on this occasion that we received a curt signal from Portsmouth: 'Cease firing. Your shells are landing in Chichester.' We expected an inquiry but heard no more, so perhaps nobody was hurt.

There was one lovely day when several of us took the motorboat to Wootton Creek and had a superb walk in the country, a swim in somebody's pool and some gorgeous beer in the Sloop Inn. I had almost forgotten what peacetime was like. Sadly, when we returned on board we heard that one of our sailors, A.B. Seddon, had been bathing over the side, dived in off the forecastle and was never seen again. He was our second casualty of the commission.

And the patrols continued in their rather uneventful way until 28 August, when we were back at Chatham for another boiler clean. This was all most civilized! I got away for forty-eight hours, as far as Cheshire to comfort my parents who were in good form, as I had survived so far and my brother, who was now a lieutenant in the Royal Engineers, was in West Africa on the way to Burma. Faith made her way from Southend and we had a drink or two on board in the evening before we left again.

Up North Again

Then it was one more patrol and to sea again on 8 September – back to horrible Scapa Flow! Our Captain (D) in *Saumarez* came with us arriving on Sunday the 10th. Ominously, we picked up arctic clothing from the depot ship, and it looked as though we should soon be back again in the frozen, wind-swept north. And so we were. To sea again on the 16th with the battleship *Rodney*, the cruiser *Diadem* and a couple of small aircraft carriers, *Campania* and *Striker*. The force went off to cover yet another Russian convoy – JW 60. The weather was very bad indeed with gales and huge seas. For some reason we were recalled to Scapa with correspondence, and actually had a night in after another struggle to secure to our buoy after refuelling. Next day it was off to screen the *Duke of York*, then to Dundee to pick up a submarine. Dundee was always a good place to visit. The natives were friendly and some of them took me to a real bit of old music hall to see and hear the immortal Nellie Wallace who must, I felt, have performed during the Boer War. The only trouble about such evenings was that one tended to drink a lot.

On our return to Scapa on 24 September, I heard that I was to be relieved. Sure enough, two days later John Cunningham arrived, to my delight. He was a nice enough fellow – I believe a 'grounded' aviator. There wasn't much time to turn the ship over before we left on the next operation, so both of us went off on this one. This time it was an air operation to mine and attack shipping in the Frohavet area of northern Norway. The carriers were *Trumpeter* and *Fencer*. What a lot of air we had at last! From our point of view, these outings were dull, and one could only try to count the aircraft out and back. The whole show took eight days of dismal weather, and we returned to Scapa (for the last time, for me) on 5 October.

South Again

After a few farewell parties I got away on Saturday the 7th, sad to leave a good (and lucky) ship, but delighted to see the last of that benighted part of the world. The journey south was tedious. Having nearly missed the only boat to the mainland, thanks to a farewell party, I enjoyed the short but choppy passage to Scrabster, whence one took transport to catch the train at Thurso. I had the somewhat stuffy company of Christopher Wake-Walker (who travelled with his sword) on the long run down to Inverness. The scenery was superb, but I wished it would move past rather faster. After a night in Inverness, having missed the usual connection, it was Perth,

Crewe and interminable waits on cold draughty stations for the final lap to West Kirby and three weeks leave.

Train journeys in wartime were unique experiences, better not repeated. I spent a few days with my parents at a cottage at Llangernyw in Wales where it was wonderfully peaceful, though it rained a lot. Then to London to call on the Admiralty about my next job. I was assured that I'd get a destroyer. Some culture in the way of ballet with Faith, and an eye check-up with a very distinguished oculist (he did Winston Churchill's eyes as well as mine) who had been in France with my father in 1914-18. All seemed well. A week or so back with my parents, spent mostly asleep. The next appointments arrived by mail, to a handful of courses before going back to sea.

A week's radar course at Portsmouth was useful and enabled me to see a few friends. An anti-submarine course in Scotland turned out to be somewhat hilarious thanks to some of the participants, notably one Tom Boyd, a large and imperturbable Yorkshire man who in private life owned a fleet of Hull trawlers and had collected a DSO in coastal forces. We all assembled in dreary Dunoon in the rain and 'proceeded' to Campbeltown by bus. This entailed a long slow progress up one side of Loch Fyne and down the other, then all the way down the Mull of Kintyre, which seemed to stretch as far as the Trans-Siberian Railway, and to be as interesting. Nothing could be seen through the rain-swept bus windows. But we stopped at such places as Ardrishaig, Inveraray and Machrihanish for refreshment (whisky), and also at a couple of places known only to Tom Boyd, where more very special whisky, at that time unobtainable in the outside world, was produced. We all lurched into Campbeltown tired and garrulous.

The course consisted of several days at sea in various converted yachts, one commanded by dear old Henry Trefusis, last seen in 1941 before *Greyhound* was sunk, but much changed by his experience. We 'attacked' tame submarines by day and in the evenings went to the pubs or the cinema. There was much speculation about our next appointments. Poor Tom Boyd received notice that he was to command a 'target-towing Town', i.e. an old ex-American four-stacker named after some town common in the US and the UK, and used to tow targets for big-ship practice shoots. What ignominy for a fire-eater! One or two others had similar 'disappointments' but nothing came through yet for me. The return trip was a great improvement – a steamer to Wemyss Bay and an evening in Glasgow (the only one I ever spent there) with a comfortable sleeper on the train to Liverpool. Waiting in the hotel for the train, I remember meeting the redoubtable Colin Maud, sole survivor of the party left on board the *Somali* when she was sunk off Kola Inlet, and recently the imperturbable beach master at Arromanches during the Normandy landings. He had an enormous black beard, which seemed to cover everything but his eyes.

The next course was convenient but demanding – the Tactical Course in Liverpool, run by that formidable figure, Captain G.H. Roberts. A simulated convoy battle on the floor of the school was as exciting as the real thing and a good deal more confusing. The Wren assistants were most knowledgeable but daren't help you much when you were surrounded by the 'fog of war', conflicting signals, sightings, explosions and information pouring in from all directions. This was really good training for command. I think it was now that I also did a damage control course in London, quite different in style. Captain Hill, who ran it, believed that we all needed a rest (which was true), and though most instructive, it was also gentlemanly and we spent some time discussing problems in the Red Cow, a pub at Baron's Court.

After that, there was a current affairs course, which was a waste of time and can only have been insisted upon by the politicians. Its whole tenor was socialist, run by the Army Bureau of Current Affairs who might have been better employed in the front line. We were encouraged to start 'discussion groups' in our ships, and reports were to be made. I doubt if many active ships did anything about it. I certainly didn't.

The next week, spent on leave, was a memorable one in my life because I went off to stay with Faith's parents at Llangollen. She was there on compassionate leave from the VADs to look after her mother who was ill. On Saturday, 2 December 1944, I was rash enough to propose matrimony while sitting on a crate of beer, which we were bringing up the hill from the pub. She was unwise enough to accept, so we were engaged. I hadn't really meant to marry for a year or two yet, but the competition seemed rather fierce and it was now or never. So we had a few days of bliss before a telegram arrived from the Admiralty ordering me to report to Captain (D) Rosyth for an appointment.

I got up there on the 12th, and to my delight found I was to command the *Valorous*, a fine First World War destroyer, modernized and in good shape. She had served in the Baltic in 1919-20 and spent most of the war to date on the east coast of England. Her pendant numbers were L 00, and she was always known as 'Lucky Loo'. Perhaps, then, a third lucky ship for me. Having been converted for an anti-aircraft role, she belonged to the Rosyth Escort Force and was usually employed escorting coastal convoys between the Firth of Forth and Sheerness.

My predecessor was Benjy Macleod whom I knew well from Dartmouth days. Benjy had everything. He was tall, good-looking, clever and athletic. He had what later became known as 'charisma'. His father was a well-known rugby football international. Benjy had been chief cadet captain at Dartmouth. He had a lovely Scandinavian wife. But there was a flaw somewhere in his character. He was a gambler and among other things couldn't resist the thrill of smuggling duty-free liquor. My wardroom (later) told me that he had some of the dockyard police bribed, and when the weather was thick, he would land such items in the boat, across to the house where he was living. He ran a greyhound in the local races and was a dashing ship handler. A hard act to follow. After the war, he left the Navy for some reason and went to South Africa where he was jailed for smuggling uncut diamonds.

The wardroom were a good lot and the ship's company admirable. Peter Deane was first lieutenant, quiet and efficient. Tiny Pettit a memorable RNVR number two, and Gellatly, the chief, was one of the old school and could fix anything. The ship herself was most comfortable, having been built in 1917 as a flotilla leader. Consequently I had a large brass bedstead in my cabin and a bath, which was heated by an extraordinary conglomeration of steam pipes and valves, which were only understood by my excellent servant, Edney, a three-badge able seaman, also of the old school. In fact *Valorous*, having been re-boilered and re-armed, still had an excellent turn of speed, good radar and a modern bridge. No canvas dodgers for me. I thought myself very lucky.

Furthermore the Rosyth Escort Force routine was regular and not too arduous – a far cry from the constant emergencies of earlier days or the unrelenting sea-time of the Home Fleet at Scapa. As a rule, one escorted a coastal convoy from the Firth of Forth to the Thames, put in at Sheerness, then brought another back to the Forth. Next time, it was a shorter run to the Humber, then back to Rosyth. After a few cycles like this, one got a boiler clean. It was essential to be on good terms with Gwyneth Goad, a super-efficient second officer, WRNS, who ran the schedule for Captain (D). The latter was one of the many 'characters' in the area, John Ruck-Keane. He was a piratical man with a Drake type beard and he either loved you or hated you. In the former case, you could do little wrong, in the latter you were in for all kinds of trouble. It was said that he held 'officers' defaulters' and that in most of his ships, one officer or another was usually under arrest.

Tom Boyd soon got on the hated list, in his old four-stacker. John R-K got on board without a proper greeting – indeed nobody was around at all. Having raised merry hell, he stomped away threatening the direst penalties if he were not greeted properly next time. Tom set up a good spy system in the dockyard, reporting Rucker's every move. So next time Tom got ample warning and when the great man arrived on the gangway, he was met by a full piping party, the Officer of the Watch in a sword, which he had borrowed from somewhere, and Tom in his best suit. As soon as the reception party had finished saluting, a steward clad in a spotless white tunic materialized from nowhere with a glass of champagne, merrily bubbling. It was risky but it worked. Tom was on the loved list thereafter. Another character was 'Uncle Cyril' Coltart, of whom more later. He was an ex-submariner and a horseracing fan and I was told that, years after the war, he lay on his deathbed watching Ascot on the television, wearing an appropriate grey top hat and sipping a last glass of champagne. There were numerous destroyers of First World War vintage in the force, and nearly all the COs were in their first commands and within a year or two of my own time. Thus, one had many friends and a lot of competition.

I took over from Benjy on 14 December, but *Valorous* was in dock so I took a trip south in the *Wallace* as a passenger to get the hang of the thing. These convoys were quite unlike those in the Atlantic or Russia. Because of the heavily mined areas all down the coast, the ships, usually 30 to 40 small coasters or colliers, proceeded in two long lines, keeping inside the narrow swept channels, which were marked by buoys all the way down. It sounds easy enough, but what with fogs, bad weather, cross currents and rather unruly ships, there were often problems, which made life interesting. Until recently, there hadn't been much enemy activity and I had the feeling that it was all rather too relaxed. But lately the Germans were perking up a bit and were sending E-boats over to the southern end of the run with mines and torpedoes, and U-boats to the deeper waters off Scotland. But it was comforting to be so near to friendly ports, especially after that cut-off feeling in the Kola Inlet area where even the friendly port was hostile in a sinister way.

On *Wallace*'s arrival at Sheerness I was able to meet Faith in London and go back with her to Wales where I was nearly shot to death going after pheasants with Martin Whitworth who only had one eye. He was the brother of Admiral 'Jock'

Whitworth who, having once been my captain in the *Rodney* was now my C-in-C at Rosyth. It was all getting quite matey. I got back to *Valorous* on Boxing Day, to find the efficient Peter Deane had everything in hand. Such are the joys of command, as opposed to being executive officer.

After a few practices on 27 December, we left on the 28th with a Sheerness-bound convoy – FS 81. Normally each convoy had only two escorts, and sailed in two long lines with the senior officer of the escort ahead and the junior (usually me) astern. Apart from being there to protect the merchant ships from enemy action, we had to try to keep them in the right channel and as far as possible closed up so that they were not strung out over miles of ocean. This was not always easy, especially in bad weather. You would close a straggler and bellow at him to try to put on a bit of speed, being tactful and, when possible, humorous. In fog, even with radar, things sometimes got quite tricky, but it was fun. By day, there was little likelihood of enemy action from the air. Their air force now barely existed. Their destroyers no longer came over as they had in the early days.

Our own shore stations were actually able to keep better track of our convoy than we were ourselves, and I once received a signal in the middle of a black night, informing me that three of my flock were aground on the Haisborough shoal. The first part of January passed in this way without much incident.

Rosyth

So it wasn't until 28 January that F[aith] and I went to Rosyth and installed ourselves in the Officers' Club. This was rather a raucous place with frozen pipes.

Our bedroom was only one half of a larger one, which had been divided by thin plasterboard to increase accommodation. To clean one's teeth one had to make one's way through the bar and dance floor. I wondered what my great grandfather, who had been hereabouts a hundred years ago, would have made of it. However, there was nowhere else to go and it was 'home' for the present.

The first couple of convoy cycles passed without much incident. I distinguished myself on going alongside the *Pytchely* in Immingham by putting a little hole in her forecastle with my anchor. The conditions were tricky, with a strong wind and awkward tide, but I should have done better than that. I hied over to call on her captain to apologise, aware that this was the formidable Gronow Davis, Captain (D21), an old destroyer man. He was a hugely fat man and was really very nice about it, plying me with an enormous gin at 10.30 in the morning (later, I was told, Gronow Davis went east to fight the Japanese but got a form of DTs in which he heard himself threatened personally by the Emperor Hirohito. He (GD) was invalided home, but died on the way). Anyhow, I think the 'Pytchleys' were pleased as they got a day or two in harbour to patch up. *Lucky Loo* wasn't even scratched. But it was embarrassing.

During our brief spell in Rosyth between convoys I found that Faith had got us some rooms in Dunfermline, a few miles out of Rosyth. Far from ideal, but a better bet than the club. Fortunately there were several officers living around there, one of whom had a car. As 'Uncle' Cyril, in addition to being captain of the base, was regional petroleum commissioner, and I had to be able to return any time at short notice, petrol was not a problem.

E-Boat Encounter

It wasn't until 21 February, with convoy FS 34 [FS 134?], known as Muskrat, that I ran into a spot of bother with the enemy who had been active lately laying mines down our route. On this occasion, we were between Immingham and Sheerness, going south, and spread out as usual over several miles. The senior officer, in *Verdun*, was ahead, I was bringing up the rear and a little after 0100 there were several heavy explosions somewhere up ahead in the convoy. After a while, it became clear that at least two ships were sinking, and it was important to know the cause – mine or torpedo. I closed one of the stricken vessels, and they reported that they had been hit by a torpedo from one of a number of E-boats, which were still around.

By now, we were a long way behind the rest of the convoy, which was steaming along in two lines with *Verdun* somewhere away ahead. A nasty decision had to be made. If I stopped to pick up the survivors from the *Goodwood* (a coaster of about 3,000 tons) I would leave the rest of the convoy naked to the enemy. So, very reluctantly, I had to drop our Carley Floats right by the wreck, call for a rescue boat from Immingham and tell the survivors that help would be on the way. With that, we raced off to rejoin the convoy.

We arrived just in time. There were several E-boats milling around, ready to fire again. The situation then became 'mouvementé'. A lot of tracer fire from both sides and then quite a shattering explosion in our boiler room which at first I could only imagine was a torpedo; light guns couldn't have done it. On these occasions there nearly always seems to be an ear-splitting escape of steam, which certainly happened now and didn't help one to think clearly. We were stopped in the water, a nice target for our own erstwhile targets. But after a few minutes of all kinds of gunnery they shoved off and were no more seen. And, of course, we couldn't pursue them.

We suffered one man killed and two seriously wounded. Unfortunately, the surgeon lieutenant was sick ashore, but the sick berth attendant did very well indeed. On investigation, we found that we had been struck by a 5" shell, which had come from one of the big merchant ships in the convoy, which must have mistaken us for the enemy in the melee. I expect they still think they got a good shot in. After getting under way again, l had to stay with the convoy until night and then peeled off in a hurry to the nearest port, Harwich, which I knew well of old. The wounded had to be got ashore to hospital without delay. Of course, down came a thick fog to make the entrance difficult, but we got in and landed our men who recovered later. We were lucky we didn't lose more. It was all a small matter, but I still remember the joy of sinking into a hot bath, surrounded by steam provided by the admirable Edney, and reflecting on an action which had been only fairly satisfactory. Next day we took another convoy to Rosyth without incident although *Vanity's* convoy in the opposite direction lost a ship by U-boat torpedo.

Repairs to the shell damage took a couple of weeks, so we had some more leave, unexpected and enjoyable. I spent most of it at home, in Dunfermline, where it was cold. I was summoned to see Admiral Whitworth to report on the action, and was gratified when he said I had done the right things. Indeed, after that I even found myself in John Ruck-Keene's good books, and ended up with another 'mention in despatches'.

The Last Convoys

When we got back on the convoy cycles we found that things were warming up quite a bit. The E-boats were having their final fling at the south end of the run, and north of the Humber the new Type XXIII U-boats were appearing, with their high underwater speed and sophisticated torpedoes. We had several alarms, and spent a lot of time hunting echoes, which may or may not have been the real thing. Our sister the *Viceroy* was sure she had sunk one in the Firth of Forth, and the recorder readings were so good that Ruckers went out to the spot, which was marked by a buoy. Another couple of patterns of depth charges were dropped and, lo and behold! up came a rubber raft with some unbroken bottles of brandy in it, undoubtedly of U-boat origin. She was later identified as *U 1274*. On the other hand, the Germans had scored by sinking the Free French destroyer *La Combattante* along the route probably by mine. As April progressed, it was evident that the war in Europe was nearing its end, though the U-boats kept at it until the last moment. We were kept pretty busy but I managed to get in a few games of golf in between convoys. In those days, my wife used to carry my bag. We had all kinds of weather – sunny and clear, fogs or very rough with that uncomfortable chop that you get in the North Sea. Signal received from an unknown trawler, who read our pendant numbers and enquired, 'Have you an Able Seaman Murgatroyd on board?' Reply: 'No, but we have a Blenkinsopp.' Very witty. We got back to Rosyth with our last convoy on 29 April.

VE Day

VE Day was a week later and there was a pleasant pause while we waited to see what would happen next. Celebration of the end of the war in Europe was relatively mild in Rosyth. There was still a chance that war might drag on for a while at sea or in Norway. Indeed, the last merchant ship sinking of the war occurred the day before VE Day, just in the entrance to the Firth of Forth. So I'd been with it to the end.

Liberation of Norway

Then word went around that the Rosyth Escort Force was to 'liberate' Norway, and there was much speculation about which ships would go. Being in Ruck-Keene's good books, I was lucky (so was Tom Boyd). On 12 May, we embarked two or three tons of stores, some soldiers equipped with walkie-talkies and, eventually, Captain Lord Teynham, RN, who was to be the senior naval officer, Kristiansand (South). Next morning, *Valorous* and *Venomous* (John Prideaux) embarked a German naval pilot with charts of the minefields off the Norwegian coast, and off we set at twenty knots for Kristiansand. Early next morning, 14 May, we rendezvoused with some German minesweepers at the entrance to the swept channel and felt our way along the coast. We were, of course, at action stations, prepared for a nasty reception in case the local command wanted to go out in a blaze of glory. On the approach, we could see some very large coast defence guns, reputed to have been taken from the *Scharnhorst*'s sister ship the *Gneisenau*, which had been written off after mine and bomb damage. But everything went quietly as we entered Kristiansand fjord at 1800 to find a group of quite large, camouflaged merchant ships at anchor, and a large number of U-boats, minesweepers and small craft at Marviken, around the corner. Hoisting a large Norwegian flag as well as our White Ensign at the fore and a Commodore's Broad pennant at the yardarm, I found a convenient anchorage not far from the jetty.

Almost at once, a stream of Norwegians appeared in small boats, giving us a pretty good welcome in rather a restrained Scandinavian way. I went ashore with Teynham, to get in touch with the powers that were – Norwegian, German or British. The latter consisted of a few hundred Special Air Service men, commanded by Brigadier Mike Calvert, long known as 'Mad Mike', with a distinguished record in the war in Burma. The SAS had been flown in about four days earlier and had already got a fair grip of the situation, though vastly outnumbered. It turned out that there was a division of German soldiers – some 15,000 men, a lieutenant general, a vice-admiral with 26 U-boats, and no less that 40,000 Russian prisoners of war in a camp nearby. The Norwegians were already rounding up the 'Quislings' for summary justice, and cropping the hair of such ladies as had been over-friendly with the Germans. There were quite a lot of these and at one stage we received a rather presumptuous invitation from the U–boat base to meet some of them. No reply.

I didn't like to be away from the ship too long, so I returned on board, leaving Teynham ashore to make his contacts. In due course he returned in a Norwegian boat manned (among others) by some nice-looking blonde girls. He asked them down to my cabin for a drink, together with some civic dignitaries.

Surrender

Almost as an afterthought, he told me that he had arranged for a German surrender delegation to repair on board in half-an-hour's time. This didn't give us much time to set up a suitable venue for such high-priced visitors, ex-enemy or no. Teynham thought they'd never make it on time anyhow. But, being German, they were on the dot and I had to keep them kicking their heels on the quarterdeck while we cleared away the Norwegians, the girls, the drinks and the tables.

It was quite a moment. The Germans were, as always, punctilious, correct, straight-backed, and poker-faced though clearly crestfallen (mixed though the metaphor may be). There was no question of resistance and they were going to cooperate. Later we found that the Navy, at any rate, were half-expecting to join us against the Russians.

In general, as had already been arranged by Mike Calvert, the Germans were to keep their arms and take care of their own discipline while they evacuated the town and started on the road trip to Oslo, and thence back to prisoner of war status in Germany. So off they went in their trucks. The SAS, being clever people, set up a roadblock several miles out of town and stripped them of all forms of 'loot' – liquor, fur coats, binoculars, cameras, and so forth. We lived for several days on champagne and liquor from all over Europe.

Next day we had a similar surrender meeting for the U-boat flotilla. There were twenty-six in all. I still have some numbers: *U 281, 299, 369, 212, 1163* (Type VII C); *U 2321, 2325, 2334, 2335, 2337, 2350, 2353, 2354, 2361, 2363* (Type XXIII); and *U 2529* (Type XXI). The Type XXIII and XXI were the very latest, streamlined and very fast underwater. We were indeed lucky that they had hardly been in service long enough to affect the war at sea.

I walked around some of them and was tremendously impressed with their equipment, their cleanliness, and the high morale of the officers and men. This was indeed remarkable considering the appalling losses they had suffered (something like four out of five of all U-Boat men). They had a superb rest camp set-up with nothing spared in the way of comforts – far better than anything we ever saw – and were treated as heroes, something that didn't seem to happen much at our end. They wanted to join us to fight the Russians whom they regarded as barbarians. I wonder whether they were aware of their own performance in the concentration camps. Our own SAS troops certainly were, having recently been through Belsen, which did not endear them to our present prisoners.

Thus we had no compunction in playing a rather dirty trick on them a few days later. Enough crews arrived from England to take the U-boats away. On the pretext of some announcement or other, all the German crews were got up on deck without warning. They were not allowed below again, and the boats in due course went off to the UK with no danger of being scuttled or destroyed (c.f. Scapa Flow in 1919!). In fact, one went to the Russians, one to the Norwegians, one to the Americans and one to the British, and the rest were eventually sunk in deep water off the Hebrides.

The Russian prisoners were another problem, fortunately not one for the Navy. 40,000 were a lot to look after. I never discovered who fed them. Many got hold of wood alcohol and drank themselves to death. German guards shot a few when they tried to break out. We were told that many had no desire to return to the USSR, suspecting no doubt the fate which awaited them. But in due course they were cowed by the commissars who wasted no time, and I believe they were all returned to Stalin's cold embraces.

The Norwegians were, naturally, pretty friendly. Once things settled down a bit and it was clear there would be no trouble from Germans or Russians we got little sleep – Norwegians only sleep in the winter, it seems.

In a way, it was hard being a recently married man. I liberated a monstrous BMW motorbike from the Germans and was able to get around the countryside a bit at the price of a few white hairs and knuckles. To tell the truth, running it on those curvy roads scared me rigid and I never got it up to full throttle.

The days were busy as we got things sorted out. But there were many parties in the evenings. One I particularly remember was a stag party at the SAS mess, which had been established on the top floor of a block of flats. There was a memorable gathering of wild men. Mike Calvert who had been a Chindit in Burma, blowing things up. Colonels Paddy Mayne, Esmond Baring and Miller-Mundy, all well-known characters, and Roy Farran, a major who had once been Montgomery's ADC and after the war couldn't stop fighting and went to Israel (on whose side, I forget). I believe he later farmed in Saskatchewan, which should have cooled him down a bit. There was a lot of champagne and lobsters as usual. In some juvenile horseplay, Calvert got a large black eye, which he had to take to call on the general in Oslo the following day. I don't suppose General Urquhart minded. This was followed by some rowdy attempts to throw sandbags from the balcony onto a jeep far below. This turned out to be the brigadier's. At this stage some sentries below, sensing a serious disturbance, fired a few shots. I retired to the inner sanctum.

It was about now that I got what was called a 'quasi-permanent' acting half-stripe, which at last lifted me out of the humble rank of lieutenant. So many contemporaries in the other services were majors or colonels or wing commanders that it had become rather galling, especially as regards the pay, observing that many of us were in command of fair sized ships. The Admiralty were slow to do anything about it, reluctant, I am sure, to find themselves top-heavy after the war.

There were two other ceremonies of note during our stay. Norwegian National Day on 17 May was a great celebration during which we marched through the town with fixed bayonets and listened to long, incomprehensible speeches, followed by some splendid parties late into the night.

Then there was the funeral of some German soldiers whose car had overturned on a bend in the road. It was very well done by the Norwegians at a little, simple chapel with a violinist playing some haunting music from Grieg. That tune stays with me still. We all felt sad for those fellows who had survived everything else. Otherwise, one hadn't much sympathy for the rest of them as one walked around the various barracks and posts, littered with the debris of a defeated army and smelling as always of stale cigar smoke. I picked up a Luger and a radio as a bit of loot. The radio never worked very well and eventually I threw away the Luger, which I could see no use for. It would fetch a good price today.

On 26 May, we left Kristiansand for Bergen, having embarked our friends the 2nd SAS. Starting at 0300, the trip took all day and was most enjoyable. The fjords were lovely although some of the channels were tricky. Next day, it was back to Kristiansand. I was glad to be back as I had made some good Norwegian friends there, especially Asbjorn Asbjornsen, with whom sadly, I have lost touch.

HMS *Tetcott*

On arrival in Kristiansand I received the startling news that I was to be relieved and was to take command of the *Tetcott*, evidently destined for the Japanese war. So I'd been right over my hasty marriage! My relief, Humphrey Barbary, arrived on 1 June, not very pleased to be taking over an old ship, no matter how efficient, which was obviously bound for the scrap yard ere long. Perhaps Their Lordships thought he needed a rest, though they hadn't given me any.

So, after mustering the Confidential Books, signing some papers and giving a farewell party, I left *Lucky Loo*, and embarked in the *Vivien* for passage to Rosyth on 4 June. After a night in Stavanger we arrived home on 6 June and I embraced my waiting wife, made some farewell calls on dignitaries from Admiral Whitworth downwards and set off for Portsmouth.

The only echo from *Valorous* was a plaintive letter from Naval Stores asking for an explanation why twelve pairs of seaboot stockings had been stowed in the boiler room, where we had written them off as destroyed by shellfire, together with a few other items we were short of. I never replied.

I assumed command of the *Tetcott* on 12 June. She was a very trim 'Hunt' class destroyer, about three years old, and had served in the Mediterranean towards the end of my time there. She had a good record and an interesting motto: 'Fayth hath no fear'. It was somewhat appropriate to my already long-suffering wife, but hardly accurate in the present context. In those days, the first captain of a ship with a new name had a say in such things as badges and mottos, and I believe this one stemmed from Richard Rycroft. I remember sending in a splendidly wild suggested badge for the *Savage*, designed by a girl friend, but it was not accepted.

Off to the East

We were due to sail on 29 June 1945 for the East and the war with the Japanese, and the expectation was that we'd get there in time for the projected invasion of Malaya. So it looked like a long separation from our families. We all had a couple of days leave, but otherwise things were pretty busy storing, ammunitioning and so forth. Faith came to dinner on the evening before sailing and we said farewell. Rather disconcertingly, she reappeared a little while before we sailed, having talked some boat coxswain into it. I was on my dignity, thinking it not proper especially as we were out at a buoy and nobody else's wife could pay a farewell call. So we parted coolly – might it have been for the last time? When I left at 1830, she had to go 'home to mum' because of course we had nowhere to live.

Actually, it was going to be a while anyhow before *Tetcott* got back into the war because it had been decided that we should stop in Gibraltar dockyard and, among other things, fit some extra light automatic weapons to repel Kamikazes.

These included a 40mm Bofors right on top of my day cabin. Somehow, all this turned into a fairly major refit, and I was anxious that we might miss the invasion. I would have liked to help kick the Nips out of anywhere – but was also feeling the separation of a newly married sailor.

It never came to that, and my command of this fine ship turned out to be another of life's anticlimaxes. We were still in Gibraltar when the Bombs were dropped on Japan. We remained there for VJ Day, the surrender and for several weeks after that, there being no urgency now to get us to sea while decisions were awaited as to our future.

Eventually it became clear that we were not to go east, but complete a full refit and return to the UK. This was sad professionally but most welcome personally. So we were not to be separated for long after all, and survival seemed likely. The waiting period in Gibraltar was tedious in one way, but fun in another. We moved out of the ship, which had become very hot in the dock, and took up residence in New Camp, an RAF establishment near the pens. It was badly run; discipline was at a low ebb. The airmen didn't care about anything but the date of their return home. When I was told that I had to ask a rather rat-like corporal for permission to get a boat across to one of the ships, I nearly exploded.

It was quite obvious to us all before the general election that the bulk of the conscripts would vote Labour – not that it was unreasonable at all in the climate of the times; but it was strange that Churchill and the Conservatives were taken by surprise when it happened. Not long before I left, there were some army sports at which the GOC got three boos instead of three cheers after the prize giving. That was the tedious side. But Jack Cox of the *Ledbury* (our chummy ship, in a like situation) and I had a wonderful rest, swimming, sailing, playing tennis and visiting the Wrennery for cooling drinks. I have always liked Gibraltar.

Two characters from the 'Rock' come to mind. A tall lean paymaster captain, with his four gold and white stripes on each arm, had a rather mean and acidic expression on his face and was known as: 'Arsenic and Gold Lace', after a popular play then current.

Another paymaster, a highly qualified lieutenant commander and lawyer in private life, was known as the 'Boozy Barrister'. I happened to be one of the members of a court martial on a sailor accused of desertion. Early in the proceedings, the 'BB' who was representing the accused man raised a 'plea in bar' – consternation. The president had to adjourn the court while the deputy judge advocate turned to the books to find out what it was.

One evening we were bidden to dinner at the 'Mount' with the admiral – Victor Crutchley. He looked like a Victorian with a full, reddish beard, a portly figure with a Victoria Cross from Ostend in 1918. His and his wife's conversation concerned only horses, and I soon ran out of points of human contact. Dinner included a brief interruption for the 'Ceremony of the Keys':

> A knock on the door.
> 'Halt, who goes there?'
> 'The Keys.'
> 'Who's Keys?'
> 'King George's Keys.'
> 'Advance, Keys and give the countersign!'

It wasn't until 16 October that after a few days at sea for trials in gorgeous sunny weather, I set sail at last for home. It was an odd feeling steaming at night with scuttles open and all lights on. A whole new life seemed to lie ahead. After a nice landfall at the Lizard, we steamed through the Needles Channel and arrived at Portsmouth dockyard at 0800 on 20 October 1945. The war was over for me.

There wasn't much of a hero's welcome. Half-a-dozen wives and a handful of scruffy dockyard mateys. But who cared?

END

Editor's Historical Note

The limitations of the fleet's air defence that Alec mentioned were just one manifestation of the problems faced by the Royal Navy when Britain declared war on Germany in September 1939. Interwar budget cuts, international treaty restrictions governing the size of most warship categories, together with the steady erosion of dockyard infrastructure all played their part. A cautious rearmament programme commenced from 1934 but the Royal Navy was to face a Kriegsmarine (German War Navy) whose ships were generally faster and more modern but far less numerous. There was no likelihood of engaging in a large-scale fleet action with Germany similar to Jutland in 1916, so in 1939 it was a matter of fighting a German guerrilla offensive against maritime trade including magnetic mines laid by aircraft, destroyers, and U-boats and this was initially devastating. Countermeasures of the type Alec described largely neutralised this threat and the Germans missed their best opportunity to overwhelm British ports with a mass deployment the following year when Britain faced possible invasion. Despite the wartime press calling this period 'The Phoney War', the reality was one of intense discomfort and danger for naval personnel.

On 3 April 1940, German troop transports sailed from Germany in the opening stage of Operation Weserübung – the invasion of Norway. The 'Phoney War' was finally over. By then, the British were on the point of executing Operation Wilfred, a plan to mine the Norwegian Leads and disrupt the vital supply of Swedish iron ore to Germany. On 9 April 1940, German troops landed at points along the Norwegian coast achieving complete surprise and encountering the only significant setback at the Battle of Drøbak Sound, where the Norwegians sank the heavy cruiser *Blücher* and badly damaged the heavy cruiser *Lützow* thus thwarting the German naval attack on Oslo. Admiral of the Fleet Sir Charles Forbes' Home Fleet was initially wrong-footed because the British Naval Intelligence Division misled him about German intentions. The German B-Dienst service was reading many British codes and deducing British movements by reading the strength and direction of their signals, giving the Kriegsmarine a clear run to their objectives at Narvik, Trondheim, Bergen, Kristiansand, and Oslo. Shortly afterwards a significant naval victory was achieved by Royal Navy warships at Narvik where the Germans lost most of their valuable destroyers and all of their naval support although it proved impossible to capitalise on this because there were no soldiers available to attack the town. The failed Allied operation at Aandalsnes was part of a pincer movement intended to capture the heavily defended port of Trondheim by landing troops north and south of the city. To complete the pincer the Allies landed at Namsos but for a variety of reasons, including overwhelming German air superiority, they decided to evacuate all forces on 28 April. *Griffin* was engaged in the subsequent re-embarkation between 3 May and 4 May 1940. Then, events elsewhere took a turn for the worse as German panzers broke through the Allied line in the Ardennes Forest into Belgium and the Netherlands causing the Allies to abandon Norway altogether. Norway was a German victory but while both sides suffered heavy warship losses, the fighting had decimated the Kriegsmarine's surface fleet. *Griffin* performed an invaluable service during this campaign by intercepting the trawler *Polares*, then in the service of the Kriegsmarine. The cipher material taken by Alec's boarding party went to the government code-breakers of Bletchley Park who broke the Enigma cipher for 22-27 April 1940. Consequently, on 11 May 1940, the British read the first German Naval Enigma message of the war.[13]

Although *Griffin* missed the Dunkirk evacuation, she took part in Operation Aerial – the evacuation of troops from northwestern France. *Griffin* joined naval forces picking up troops from St. Nazaire and other Brittany ports. Aerial and the parallel Operation Cycle successfully rescued some 200,000 Allied troops along with their stores and equipment from France. The official naval historian noted that Aerial 'attracted little attention; but in some ways it was an even more convincing demonstration [than Dunkirk] of the effectiveness of sea power'.[14]

On returning to England, the initial stage of the Battle of Britain (the Kanalkampf) began. This attempt by the Luftwaffe's aircraft and Kriegsmarine's E-boats to stop shipping movements in the English Channel failed mainly because of the determination of the merchant navy crews to keep going in the face of heavy attacks. Destroyers such as *Griffin* operated from their Channel bases to protect vital merchant convoys and the floating tripwire of small miscellaneous craft kept watch for enemy shipping movements. Having to patrol in daylight inevitably meant that British ships endured many air attacks; however, most shipping losses in the Channel at this time were attributable to mines. Throughout the summer, naval flotillas made many successful night attacks in all weathers on German held invasion ports, sinking barges and bombarding port installations demonstrating that the Germans did not have control of the Channel at night. As the German plan for invading the British Isles (Operation Sea Lion) required the first wave of troops to cross at night for a dawn landing, the Royal Navy's night supremacy made their plan unworkable. The Battle of Britain was also the period of the U-boat's 'Happy Time' and marked an acute phase in the ongoing Battle of the Atlantic. This was because the underwater detection system known as ASDIC was proving disappointing, convoys lacked air cover, and many escorts were away on anti-invasion duties. Despite their small operational numbers and unreliable torpedoes, U-boat captains were wreaking havoc upon unprotected merchant shipping.

The end of August saw *Griffin* patrolling off Gibraltar where the Mediterranean had calmed down since Italian dictator Benito Mussolini's declaration of war in June 1940. In response to fears of Italian air and naval power against shipping, the Admiralty closed the Suez Canal to commercial traffic and re-routed convoys around the Cape adding 3,500 miles to the sea routes supplying India. The Middle East held great strategic importance as the Suez Canal remained a key communications link with India and the Far East. Prime Minister Winston Churchill also needed to impress America with Britain's determination to fight and thus Vice Admiral Sir Andrew Cunningham's Force H engaged the Italian Regia Marina (Italian Navy) and Regia Aeronautica off the coast of Calabria despite a British numerical inferiority. Today it is easy to forget that in 1940, Mussolini possessed a modern fleet and the fourth largest air force in the world. The battle was inconclusive but successful enough to encourage Churchill to send further reinforcements such as *Griffin* to the area. It also proved that high-level bombing had little effect upon warships.[15]

Vice Admiral Sir James Somerville handled the 'dirty job' of sinking the French Mediterranean Fleet at Mers el Kebir earlier in the year but Churchill was dissatisfied with the extent he had pressed home the attack. Alongside the seizures of French shipping in British held ports, there was enough damage inflicted to ensure that the Kriegsmarine would not recover their depleted naval strength at French expense and make Sea Lion a viable operation of war. However, the remnants existed in sufficient strength to ensure considerable caution in future British dealings with the French. The British expedition to Dakar was a bungled attempt to rally the French African Empire to the Free French cause doomed by the arrival of a Vichy French naval squadron. British hesitancy enabled them to slip through the straits of Gibraltar and the fiasco destroyed many reputations. This was mainly due to ambiguous Admiralty orders failing to make clear how the fleet should act in such situations. In

Somerville's case, Churchill did not relent towards him until much later in the war. In the case of Sir Dudley North, Rear Admiral in Charge, Gibraltar, the admiral faced the sack and North would have to wait until after the war to recover his reputation.

Twenty-one Swordfish aircraft launched from the flight deck of *Illustrious* on the evening of 11 November 1940 began an action that sank three Italian battleships in Taranto's outer harbour. The results were not permanent but for a short time it changed the military balance in the Mediterranean more in Britain's favour than before and helped impress the Americans with her determination to fight. With British civilians only able to 'take it' during the Night Blitz, this was one of the few positive successes being offered up to the British and American public at this time. However, the Battle of Taranto's precise impact is a matter for continuing debate.[16] There is little doubt that possession of the *Eagle*, *Illustrious*, and *Ark Royal* gave the British a key advantage over the Italians who had no carriers whatsoever.

The year 1940 ended with the fleet supporting Operation Compass – the offensive against Marshal Rodolfo Graziani's army that almost swept the Italians out of North Africa. Because of Taranto, the fleet was free to run convoys across the Mediterranean relatively unhindered, provide a ferry service for troops and, as Alec described, participate in the bombardment of Bardia. By noon on the first day, thousands of Italians in Bardia were surrendering though stubborn pockets held out for a further two days. The New Year was looking brighter but things were about to change. Concerned over the Axis invasion of Greece and fearing a drive upon the Middle East from the Balkans, Churchill took valuable resources away to assist the Greeks. Compass halted as Field Marshal Sir Archibald Wavell was about to administer the coup de grace upon Graziani's shattered army. It had been a difficult decision given the need to buttress crumbling Greek resistance, and continue demonstrating British willingness to fight to the Americans.

Furthermore, with Hitler's Mediterranean intervention in support of Mussolini, the fleet would again have to contend with the Luftwaffe – in particular Fliegerkorps X, the unit *Griffin* previously encountered off Norway. The Germans soon realised that Malta was key to maintaining Generalleutnant Erwin Rommel's position in North Africa and consequently the island's ordeal by air attacks continued almost unabated from the date of the damaging attack on *Illustrious* in Malta's Grand Harbour on 16 January into February and March.

Griffin was involved in the famous night action off Cape Matapan on 28 March. The Government Code and Cypher School (GC&CS) at Bletchley Park discovered that the Regia Marina was about to attack troop convoys sailing to Greece. These were re-routed and Cunningham slipped out of Alexandria Harbour under cover of darkness with battleships *Warspite, Barham*, and *Valiant*, also taking the recently arrived carrier *Formidable* and nine destroyers. In all, the action cost the Regia Marina three large warships, two destroyers and approximately 2,400 personnel against the British loss of one Swordfish aircraft. The only disappointment was the escape of the battleship *Vittoria Veneto* but as the official historian remarked it was a 'substantial victory' and 'complete justification for the emphasis placed on efficiency in night fighting by the Royal Navy'.[17]

However, German land offensives in Cyrenaica, Greece and Yugoslavia drove all before them and it was looking as if the soldiers so recently transported from Africa might be stranded. By mid-April, Rommel had pushed beyond Compass's start line of the previous year and the port of Tobruk was under siege and only supplied with great difficulty. After an ineffective bombardment of the Axis supply port of Tripoli, British efforts were concentrated on intercepting the Axis supply ships at sea using the surface ships, submarines, and aircraft based at Malta. However, the surface ships soon withdrew from Malta owing to the parlous state of the British position in Greece leaving small numbers of strike aircraft and submarines bearing the burden of attacking the enemy supply lines for the time being. *Griffin* was also involved in the evacuation of the British Expeditionary Force from Greece to Crete from eight different harbours beginning on the night of 24-25 April. The air attacks resulted in heavy damage among the lightly armed troop transports, four of which sank after bombing. On a positive note, the Navy rescued approximately 51,000 men, representing eighty per cent of the force sent to Greece.[18]

On 20 May, the expected airborne assault on Crete began. Because the main harbours including Suda Bay pointed towards the Greek mainland and the Luftwaffe held air superiority, Cunningham had to operate his fleet from Alexandria, some 400 miles away. They successfully frustrated two German attempts to land reinforcements by sea but because the situation on land turned in favour of Germany following the loss of Maleme airfield, the War Cabinet decided on 27 May that yet another evacuation was necessary. Appreciating that the fleet had already been through a terrible ordeal and the crews were exhausted, the army commanders tried to absolve Cunningham of responsibility for carrying out the evacuation. This is when Cunningham famously remarked that the Navy would not let the Army down as abandoning the troops meant 'our naval tradition would never survive such an action'. Cunningham's ruthless drive and determination meant that 17-18,000 soldiers survived to fight another day but 12,000 fell into captivity. The cost to the Royal Navy had been heavy. One aircraft carrier, two battleships, six cruisers and seven destroyers were severely damaged with three cruisers and six destroyers sunk.[19]

A new crisis in Iraq, Iran, and Syria caused *Griffin* and other land sea and air units to avert a growing threat to the oil supply. Back in April an Axis inspired coup d'état in Iraq ousted the regent, but action by Vice Admiral G.S. Arbuthnot's East Indies Squadron and two convoys of troops put down the revolt by 1 June. However, the episode raised fears in London that the Germans had infiltrated the neighbouring French mandate of

Syria, part of the Vichy regime. In mid-May, the War Cabinet ordered preparations for an assault upon the Vichy garrisons in Syria. On 8 June, the army advanced into Syria from Trans-Jordan and Palestine with the Navy allocating three cruisers and eight destroyers to protect their seaward flank. On 15 June, naval torpedo bombers sank the French flotilla leader *Chevalier Paul* and from this point on, the British began to gain the upper hand. By 11 July, the French commander was ready to sign an armistice effectively ceding the mandate to British and Free-French control. During this campaign, another force from Aden launched Operation Chronometer – an amphibious assault on the Italian naval base at Assab in Eritrea thus eliminating the last remnants of any Italian threat against the Red Sea shipping routes.

By securing the northern and southern boundaries of the British Middle East position, the recent losses of Greece and Crete were somewhat offset. Furthermore, with the Red Sea and Gulf of Aden cleared of Axis forces, President Roosevelt was able to declare these were no longer combat zones and American shipping could proceed to the Suez Canal, thus easing the strain on stretched British shipping resources. Shortly afterwards, the War Cabinet decided to extend military action to neighbouring Iran (Persia). By 25 August, British and Commonwealth forces had seized the Iranian naval bases and oilfields and the British strategic position in the Middle East was more secure.

However, the continuing need to support the struggling Army of the Nile in the Western Desert (8th Army from September 1941) resulted in the Admiralty having to make urgent supply runs to Malta and Tobruk. *Griffin* became involved in numerous supply expeditions to Tobruk, second only to Malta in the British scale of priority. Over the 242-day-long siege (12 April-8 December) the warships carried in 34,113 troops, 34,000 tons of stores, 92 guns and 72 tanks. The 8th Army pushed Rommel back to El Agheila by the end of 1941 but maintaining their lifeline was costly, resulting in the loss of twenty-five warships and five merchant ships.[20]

The sinking of *Ark Royal* and the battleship *Barham* in November 1941, followed by the cruiser *Galatea* on 14 December were heavy blows but early in the morning of 19 December, Malta's Force K ran into a minefield laid by Italian destroyers. This resulted in the loss of the cruiser *Neptune* with almost the entire ship's company, heavy damage to two others, plus the loss of the destroyer *Kandahar* effectively bringing to an end the career of Force K and again pushing the burden of offensive operations against Axis convoys on to the Malta-based submarines and strike aircraft. That day, the Italians severely damaged the *Queen Elizabeth* and *Valiant* with limpet mines. They remained out of action for almost two years. The Axis then ran a succession of convoys transforming Rommel's previously parlous position in the desert.

On 7 December 1941, aircraft of the Imperial Japanese Navy (IJN) attacked the American Pacific Fleet at their base in Pearl Harbor, Hawaii, and America was finally at war with the Axis powers. Serious defeats followed including the sinking of the battleship *Prince of Wales* and heavy cruiser *Repulse* as Japanese forces swept into South East Asia and across the Pacific Ocean. Against this backdrop, *Griffin* left the Mediterranean and joined Somerville's newly constituted Eastern Fleet. In the waters of the Far East, the Eastern Fleet avoided direct confrontation with the IJN's formidable airpower, as there was no prospect of making good further losses to the ramshackle fleet of elderly and worn out ships that Somerville had at his disposal. Somerville worked from the secret base at Addu Atoll in the Maldives because Colombo and Trincomalee had inadequate facilities and were vulnerable to Japanese attacks.

The Battle of the Coral Sea, fought between 7 and 9 May, became the first real check to the Japanese advance as the US Navy frustrated the intended invasion of Port Moresby in New Guinea. However, the damage caused by Japanese carrier raids in the Indian Ocean raised fears of attacks upon weakly defended lines of communication between the Middle East and the Far East. Should Japan acquire the Vichy held island of Madagascar and its naval base at Diego Suarez, then the entire British position in the Middle East might be in jeopardy. *Griffin* was part of a task force sent to seize the island from the French. British and Commonwealth assault troops landed in the French rear early on 5 May taking the garrison by surprise while Fleet Air Arm aircraft from *Illustrious* and *Indomitable* attacked Madagascar's airfields and warships. The French surrendered the base on 7 May, although fighting continued in other parts of the island until September. The official historian was later to write that this success was very welcome because it had finally demonstrated a satisfactory command organisation for combined operations.[21] The Allied success in capturing Diego Suarez largely removed the danger to their lines of communication, though it is hard to gauge how realistic the Japanese threat actually was. Although Germany quickly recognised the value of Diego Suarez to the Axis cause and tried to convince their ally to take action, the Japanese refused to disclose any precise plans beyond a vague intention to station a few submarines and some auxiliary cruisers in the general area.[22]

Shortly after the Diego Suarez operation, the IJN and US Navy began massing their fleets far to the east before closing on Midway Island in the Hawaiian group. The subsequent US victory marked the end of an almost unbroken string of Japanese victories in the Far East, and henceforth Allied forces in the Far East were on the offensive. While Midway eased the pressure off the Allies in the East, the British position in the Mediterranean remained critical, as Rommel approached the peak of his success. *Griffin* returned to the Mediterranean and took part in Operation Vigorous, a failed attempt to re-supply Malta, whose position was again desperate. Back in April 1942, the island had received the George Cross to 'bear witness to the heroism and devotion of its people' in the face of extreme bombing and privations but it would be many months before the siege was lifted.[23]

While the worn-out *Griffin* was returning home, thousands of American troops were crossing the Atlantic to take part in Operation Torch – the invasion of French Morocco and French Algeria. On 2 November, *Griffin* arrived in Southampton while the Battle of El Alamein was taking place. This victory alongside the success of Operation Torch set the Afrika Korps on the road to Tunis where it was to suffer a catastrophic defeat the following year. Churchill famously wrote, 'It may almost be said, before Alamein we never had a victory, after Alamein we never had a defeat.'[24]

Alec's new ship, *Savage*, took part in the renewed Arctic convoy operations. Convoys to support the Soviet war effort were operating since the German invasion of the Soviet Union in 1941. The only viable route was over the top of German occupied Norway into the Arctic where conditions meant increased navigational and signalling difficulties because of the poor light. Loose floating ice was also a hazard for the majority of ships with bows not specifically built for such conditions. Appalling conditions took a heavy toll, with casualties from frostbite and having to live in permanently cold, wet environments. Casualties from enemy action were also high – notably when German aircraft and submarines from Norway tore convoy PQ17 apart in July 1942. No more convoys sailed until September 1942 when the next convoy, PQ18, included new escort carriers giving the merchant ships more air and antisubmarine protection. As the war progressed, the material advantage to the Soviets from the Arctic convoys declined as supply routes from Persia and across the Pacific opened up. Yet such was their symbolic importance they continued until the end of the war. Nearly a quarter of the aid given to the USSR throughout the conflict came via the Arctic.

Despite a change in German strategy away from large surface ships brought about by the Battle of the Barents Sea, the presence of battleships *Scharnhorst* and *Tirpitz* in northern waters remained a potent threat to the Arctic convoys. At this point, the *Tirpitz* was successfully immobilised by midget submarines at Altenfjord on 21 September 1943 but the *Scharnhorst* escaped. The Battle of the North Cape became the last fight by a British battleship against another battleship and it demonstrated beyond doubt the value of radar-assisted gunnery, as *Scharnhorst* had been capable of outgunning most of her opponents.[25] More convoys followed the Battle of the North Cape and, as Alec's text shows, some such as JW56A in January 1944 (where Alec found himself in the water for the first time) encountered bitter U-boat opposition. By then, the U-boats were using sophisticated acoustic torpedoes, but decoy noise-making devices such as the British Foxer helped neutralize the threat. Unfortunately, the devices also restricted the towing ship's speed and the noise revealed its position to the U-boats.

After this, *Savage* participated in Operation Overlord – the invasion of Western Europe that began with the D-Day landings off the coast of Normandy on 6 June 1944. The Anglo-American Quadrant Conference at Quebec in August 1943 approved the outline plan but Allied strategy agreed at Casablanca in early 1943 focused on clearing the Mediterranean of Axis forces including the invasion of Sicily, thus ensuring there could be no resources for a cross-Channel invasion before 1944. Another factor was the need to make the Atlantic supply routes safer for a build-up of American troops in the British Isles. Until increased merchant ship production, advances in signals intelligence, new equipment, and tactics including the use of very-long-range aircraft all combined to produce a decisive ascendancy over the U-boat in the summer of 1943, the submarines remained a major obstacle. Even then, the Battle of the Atlantic was far from over, but henceforth the U-boats would not achieve their previous levels of success.

The English Channel was much safer for Allied warships than four years previously and with heightened levels of inter-service and inter-Allied cooperation, planning was meticulous. German air and sea power was weaker but *Savage's* position out on the screen of the invasion fleet still exposed her to risk. *Savage* and other escorts fought off E-boat attacks from the ninth S-boat flotilla but the overall losses from German naval action that day were slight. The Luftwaffe mounted 260 combat sorties over Normandy on 6 June but in comparison with the enormous Allied air efforts, the German air response was feeble. Part of the German reaction was to launch a number of Fritz X and HS293 radio-controlled bombs (forerunners of modern guided missiles) at the ships but a combination of Allied air superiority and new electronic jamming equipment frustrated the attacks. Overlord reached a successful conclusion but the war was to continue for many months.

By early 1945, Germany had increasing numbers of submarines including the Type XXIII so-called elektroboats, based in Norway. These formidable submarines were faster than their predecessors, and because their snorkel devices allowed air into their powerful diesel engines they could remain submerged most of the time. Allied airborne radar was rarely able to engage and even at this very late stage of the war, the Admiralty feared that a renewed U-boat offensive with these new weapons in the Atlantic might still prejudice the European land campaign. In the event, and as with all the late generation of 'wonder-weapons', Germany was unable to manufacture enough to influence the outcome.

The formal surrender of all German forces in Norway took place at Oslo on 9 May following a series of local surrender ceremonies in Norwegian ports. These included the surrender at Kristiansand where Alec and his colleagues obtained their first close-up look at this new generation of U-boats. The wartime career of Commander J.A.J. Dennis effectively ended at Gibraltar on VJ Day. He was lucky to survive as the human cost to the Royal Navy had been heavy – 50,758 killed, 820 missing and 14,663 wounded. Mention should also be made of the Women's Royal Naval Service, sustaining 102 killed and 22 wounded. Enemy action also claimed 30,248 sailors of the British Merchant Navy.[26]

The world has changed since the end of the Second World War and the Royal Navy in which Alec and his contemporaries served has changed with it. At least one thing remains the same: 'As an island nation, our prosperity and security is totally dependent on our ability to access the sea.'[27] It seems that Britain will need men like Alec for many years to come!

End Notes

1. Newbolt, 'Drakes Drum'.
2. Hough R., *Bless Our Ship* (1991), p.13.
3. Hough, ibid, p.114.
4. Tweedie H.J. in R.H.S. Bacon's *Britain's Glorious Navy*, p.151.
5. See bibliography.
6. Winston Churchill, *The Gathering Storm*, page 524: '...but the Germans had already crossed the outer lines, and were now streaming across the causeway, which enclosed the Zuyder Zee. Could we do anything to prevent this? Luckily we had a flotilla not far away and this was immediately ordered to sweep the causeway with fire and take the heaviest toll possible of the swarming invaders.'
7. Actually sunk by *U-38*, Kapitän-Leutnant Liebe, an 'ace' who survived the war.
8. There is an interesting comment in John Colville's (Churchill's private secretary) diary, *The Fringes of Power*, for 7 August 1940: 'The First Lord told me on the telephone about 1 am that a troopship had been torpedoed off Ireland. This depressed Winston greatly, however he recovered when he heard that nearly all the men had been saved, and that there were no valuable stores on board, merely remarking that the navy was not being successful against U-boats as in the past. (We have lost much shipping lately).'
9. I have an excellent book called *Mediterranean Maelstrom* which gives the history of the *Jervis* who bore a life as charmed as our own. It is irritating that Mountbatten's *Kelly* (which really had rather an undistinguished career until she was sunk in May 1941) got all the publicity.
10. ABC, in his book, recounts how his new chief of staff, a distinguished gunnery officer, was heard to exclaim, 'Good God, We've hit her!'.

11. This was the occasion when Roden Cutler of Sydney, brother of a great friend, and later Governor of New South Wales, got a Victoria Cross.
12. It was strange that after the collapse of the Soviet Union, fifty-odd years later, my son Alan attended an Avalanche conference near Murmansk. Not long before this, the Russians had awarded us commemorative medals for the campaign (our own people never so recognised it). When he showed them my 'citation', they were all over him and plied him with vodka (but he is a TT). There is now a huge memorial up there to those who fought. Alan was able to telephone me direct from his hotel room. I wouldn't have believed it possible in 1943.
13. Sebag-Montefiore (2000), pp.73-7.
14. Roskill, *The Navy*, p.80.
15. Cunningham A.B., Report, 2643-9.
16. Farley R, 'Attack', 42-3.
17. Roskill, ibid., pp.154-65.
18. Roskill, ibid., 159-61.
19. Roskill, ibid., p.165.
20. Roskill, ibid., 166-8.
21. Roskill, ibid., 190-1.
22. Turner, Gordon-Cumming and Betzler (1961), *War in the Southern Oceans*, p.117.
23. 'On this day', BBC.
24. Churchill, *The Hinge of Fate* (1954), p.487.
25. Hore P., 'Guns' (June 2016), p.45.
26. Roskill, *The Navy*, p.423.
27. The Royal Navy's Role, *Ministry of Defence*.

Bibliography

Books

Bacon R.H.S. (ed)., *Britain's Glorious Navy*, (Odhams Press, 1942)

Bennett G.H. & Bennet R., *Hitler's Admirals*, (Naval Institute Press, Annapolis MD, 2004)

Churchill, W.S., *The Gathering Storm: The Second World War* I, (Penguin Classics, 2005)

Churchill, W.S., *Their Finest Hour: The Second World War* II, (Cassell, 1949)

Churchill, W.S., *The Grand Alliance, The Second World War* III, (Penguin Classics, 2005)

Churchill W.S., *The Hinge of Fate: The Second World War* IV, (Reprint Society, 1954)

Churchill W.S., *Triumph and Tragedy: The Second World War*, (Penguin Classics, 2005)

Colville J., *The Fringes of Power: The Downing Street Diaries, 1939-45*, (New York, W.W. Norton, 1985)

Cunningham A.B., *A Sailor's Odyssey*, (Hutchinson, 1951)

David S., *Military Blunders: The How and Why of Military Failure*, (Robinson, 1997)

Greene J. and Massignani A., *The Naval War in the Mediterranean 1940-1943*, (Frontline Books, 2011)

Griehl M., *Junkers Ju.87 Stuka*, (Airlife Publishing, Shrewsbury, 2001)

Hough R., *Bless Our Ship: Mountbatten and the Kelly*, (Coronet Books, 1991)

Ireland B., *Battle of the Atlantic*, (Leo Cooper, 2003)

Kersoudy F., *Norway, 1940*, (Collins, 1990)

Longmate N., *Island Fortress: The Defence of Great Britain 1603-1945*, (Pimlico 2001)

Mallman Showell J., *Fuehrer Conferences on Naval Affairs 1939-1945*, (Chatham, 2005)

Porch D., *The Path to Victory: The Mediterranean Theater in World War II*, (Farrar, Straus and Giroux, New York, 2004)

Roskill S., *The Navy at War 1939-1945*, (Wordsworth, 1998)

Roskill S., *The War at Sea 1939-45*, I, (HMSO, 1954)

Roskill S., *Churchill and the Admirals*, (William Morrow & Co., New York, 1978)

Sebag-Montefiore S., *Enigma: Battle for the Code*, (Cassell Military Histories, 2004)

Simpson M. (ed.), *The Cunningham Papers* (The Navy Records Society, 1990)

Smith P.C., *Critical Conflict: The Royal Navy's Mediterranean Campaign in 1940*, (Pen & Sword Maritime, Barnsley, 2011)

Spector R., *At War at Sea: Sailors and Naval Warfare in the Twentieth Century*, (Allen Lane, 2001)

Terraine J., *The Right of the Line: The Royal Air Force in the European War, 1939-1945*, (Wordsworth, 1998)

Turner L.C.F., Gordon-Cumming H.R. and Betzler J.E., *War in the Southern Oceans*, (Oxford University Press, 1961)

Weal J., *Focke-Wulf Fw 190 Aces of the Western Front*, (Osprey, 2004)

Official Publications

Naval Staff History: The Development of British Naval Aviation 1919-1945 Vol.2. (Admiralty, 1956)

Websites

Barras J., The Battle of Ceylon – 1942, *LankaLibrary Sri Lanka*, lankalibrary.com/geo/30-squadron.htm (accessed, 4 July 2016)

Battle of Madagascar, *War History Online*, warhistoryonline.com/war-articles/battle-madagascar.html (accessed 8 June 2016)

Commander Alec Dennis, *Telegraph Media Group Limited* 2008 jproc.ca/crypto/enigs3_alec_dennis.html (accessed 20 June 2016)

Hartley L.P., *The Go Between*, as quoted by *Goodreads*, goodreads.com/quotes/66426-the-past-is-a-foreign-country-they-do-things-differently (accessed 13 May 2016)

Mason G.B., HMS Gurkha Tribal Class Destroyer Service Histories, naval-history.net/xGM-Chrono-10DD-34Tribal-Gurkha1.htm (accessed 10 May 2009)

Mason G.B., HMS SAVAGE (G 20) – S-class Destroyer, naval-history.net/xGM-Chrono-10DD-55S-HMS_Savage.htm (accessed 20 April 2016)

Henry Newbolt, 'Drakes Drum,' *Poetry Soup*, poetrysoup.com/
famous/poem/8613/drakes_drum (accessed 28 June 2015)
The Torpedoes, uboat.net/technical/torpedoes.htm (accessed 24
May 2016)
Ships Hit from Convoy RA57, uboat.net/ops/convoys/convoys.
php?convoy=RA-57 (accessed 20 May 2016)

Official Web Archives

'On this day', BBC, news.bbc.co.uk/onthisday/hi/dates/stories/
april/15/newsid_3530000/3530301.stm (accessed 17 August
2016)
The Silent Service: The Royal Navy and the North African
Campaign, The National Archives, http://webarchive.
nationalarchives.gov.uk/20100709234706/http://www.cwgc.org/
northafrica/content.asp?menuid=35&submenuid=41&id=
41&menuname=The%20Silent%20Service&menu=sub
(accessed 18 August 2017)
The Royal Navy's Role: Global Trade and Security, *Ministry of
Defence*, royalnavy.mod.uk/About-the-Royal-Navy/~/media/
Files/Navy-PDFs/About-the-Royal-Navy/RN%20and%20
Global%20Trade%20Security.pdf (accessed 3 June 2016)

Newspapers, Journals & Periodicals

Bennett G.H., 'The Arctic Convoys: The Worst Journey in the
World', *BBC History Magazine*, pp.50-56
Cunningham A.B., 'Report of an Action with the Italian Fleet off
Calabria', 9 July 1940, (Cunningham's Despatch), Supplement
to *The London Gazette*, 28 April 1948
'Commander Alec Dennis visiting Bletchley Park on 15 October
2003', *News from Bletchley Park Trust*, 7 October 2003
Farley R., 'Attack on Taranto,' *Warships International Fleet Review*,
January 2011, p.42-3
Hore P., 'Guns who Played Key Part in Royal Navy's last Battleship
Fight', *Warships International Fleet Review*, June 2016, p.45
Rear-Admiral John Lee-Barber, Obituaries, *Daily Telegraph*, 22
November 1995
Levy J., 'Lost Leader: Admiral of the Fleet, Sir Charles Forbes.'
The Mariner's Mirror 88, no.2 (2002), p.190

Index